AGILE MIND, OPEN HEART

The 9 Steps for Developing Inner Leadership for a Changing World

KAMRAN TORK

BALBOA.PRESS
A DIVISION OF HAY HOUSE

Copyright © 2020 Kamran Tork.

All rights reserved. No part of this book may be used or reproduced by any means, graphic, electronic, or mechanical, including photocopying, recording, taping or by any information storage retrieval system without the written permission of the author except in the case of brief quotations embodied in critical articles and reviews.

Balboa Press books may be ordered through booksellers or by contacting:

Balboa Press
A Division of Hay House
1663 Liberty Drive
Bloomington, IN 47403
www.balboapress.com
1 (877) 407-4847

Because of the dynamic nature of the Internet, any web addresses or links contained in this book may have changed since publication and may no longer be valid. The views expressed in this work are solely those of the author and do not necessarily reflect the views of the publisher, and the publisher hereby disclaims any responsibility for them.

The author of this book does not dispense medical advice or prescribe the use of any technique as a form of treatment for physical, emotional, or medical problems without the advice of a physician, either directly or indirectly. The intent of the author is only to offer information of a general nature to help you in your quest for emotional and spiritual well-being. In the event you use any of the information in this book for yourself, which is your constitutional right, the author and the publisher assume no responsibility for your actions.

Any people depicted in stock imagery provided by Getty Images are models, and such images are being used for illustrative purposes only.
Certain stock imagery © Getty Images.

Print information available on the last page.

ISBN: 978-1-9822-4755-3 (sc)
ISBN: 978-1-9822-4756-0 (e)

Balboa Press rev. date: 05/29/2020

CONTENTS

Preface vii
Introduction 1
Understanding Your Mind 9

Chapter 1 The Mind As Master 11
Chapter 2 Understanding The Reactive Old Mind 17
Chapter 3 The Dawn of the Agile New Mind 21

Nine Steps To An Agile Mind, Open Heart 27

Chapter 4 The Tools For Transformation 29
Chapter 5 The 9-Steps 39

Bibliography of Texts, Programs, Videos and Resources 129
About the Author 133

PREFACE

Developing a Leadership State of Mind and Heart

Welcome. I am Kamran Tork, a Professional Certified Coach in Executive Leadership. For the last ten years, I have coached hundreds of business leaders about Emotional Intelligence and Self-Reflective Practices. Many of my former clients have requested a companion guide for easy future reference as workplace challenges arise. This book has been written in response to those suggestions.

My coaching sessions are based on the belief that the future requirement in leadership will be for executives who have progressively developed a "leadership state of mind and heart." By that I mean, equal attention will be given to the inner state from which a leader operates, in addition to his or her outer technical expertise. The inner state of a leader is an important contributor to his/her leadership effectiveness and therefore has a major impact on the organization's performance, as well as its financial and corporate well-being.

Firstly, it is important to understand that if leaders' actions are informed by a reactive state of mind with a dominant need for safety above all, their leadership effectiveness will be jeopardized. On the other hand, when leaders lead out of a creative state, with a primary need for purpose and vision, they will be their most effective. In his book, Mastering Leadership, Robert Anderson suggests that nearly 80% of leadership operate from a reactive state– motivated by safety - as opposed to the purpose driven creative state. This is alarming! If we refer to Maslow's Hierarchy of Needs, we see that the need for safety corresponds to the lowest rung of evolutionary development.

Questions arise such as why would a sane organization want to be led by leadership predominantly operating out of the lowest level of needs?

Secondly, the evolutionary level or inner state of maturity of a leader will determine the processes, structures and procedures implemented in that organization. Leaders who operate from the reactive state of craving safety will not support structures and policies that will empower others. It is too threatening to their own identity and ego construct and therefore they cannot appreciate more developed structures that include self-organizing.

In his book Reinventing Organizations, Frederic Laloux, correlates the inner developmental state of leaders to the structures they put in place. The least effective organizations are hierarchal and are supported by leadership dominant in command style, whereas, more effective leaders operating from a healthy inner state are proponents of self-organizing structures – what Laloux labels as "Teal Organizations." He emphasizes that a leader who inwardly operates from a need for safety will not and cannot appreciate the most evolutionary structures even if such structures benefit leadership, employees and business outcome.

The third way that the inner state of a leader matters, is how it impacts company climate. Daniel Goleman and Hay Consulting findings suggest that company climate accounts for 20-30% of employee motivation. The major factor that influences the company climate is leadership at 50% and higher. A leader that operates from a reactive state does not have mastery over his/her thoughts and emotions and thus cannot foster cohesively collaborative climates focused on shared vision. The resulting reactivity and lack of self-mastery will alienate high potentials rather than attracting them.

A state of mind trapped in the safety-oriented default mode, operating out of an automatic, reactive intellect and a dominant critical frame of mind, fosters separation, division, and conflict causing crisis both within and around the leader and his/her extended environment.

What can help facilitate a shift in a leader's stage of development or inner-state?

Robert Keegan of Harvard puts it formidably - make the subject an object of observation. What does that mean? As long as our thought process, in general, and our default thinking, in particular, is unseen by us, we are fused with it. We are it! It runs us. Only by making our thought process obvious to our awareness (the subject) can we make our reactive default thinking mind an object. That which was a subject running the show, has now turned to an object that is being looked at – much like a table in front of us – it is out there so we can see it. Wisdom traditions with their focus on creating a healthy space between the default reactive intellect (object) and the attentive "awaring" process (subject) allude to the same truth. As said in Vedanta philosophy, "Mind makes an excellent servant but a poor master". Hence the strong interest in and rise of self-reflective practices as a leadership development tool with organizations around the world.

Understand, we are not leading effectively while we operate from a speedy reactive state of mind - that is followship - not leadership.

This book and the group coaching that complement it, are designed for facilitating an inner-shift in leaders to best complement their outer competencies with inner-qualities to lend a new leadership fit to the complexities of 21st Century.

INTRODUCTION

You have probably heard sayings such as "better the devil you know," which implies that something bad but known is much better than that which is unknown.

While it may seem unreasonable and perhaps even a bit foolish to prefer the bad to the unknown, especially if the unknown offers possibilities of something better, this is a common stumbling block for many people. In truth, most will go to great lengths to re-establish their sense of well-being by unconsciously or automatically returning to a familiar setting, whether that be a place, relationship, activity, or a state of mind.

Even though a reset of this nature will restore some sense of control and equilibrium – at least for a time - the inherent danger of repeatedly falling back on the familiar or known patterns of living and thinking will create a rut so deep that you will eventually find yourself stuck. In a world that is becoming increasingly volatile, uncertain, complex, and ambiguous, if you are not moving forward, you are falling behind. This outcome is not a good one for anybody, especially for those in a leadership position.

Default Mind

Another well-known saying about the general who is always fighting the last war suggests that people are more inclined to rely solely on what has been done and they believe worked for them in the past when dealing with a new and challenging situation. This default thinking, i.e. defaulting to the familiar is habitual and reflexive because it happens within a split second and out of your conscious here and now state. In this habitual state, your default mind is analytical, critical, and judging, but it is judging based on what has occurred in the past and therefore leaves little room for agile, holistic, conscious or intentional thinking regarding what may be the reality of the present.

Let's take a step back and examine my personal experience with the default mind.

A well-known peer in the industry reached out to me to collaborate with him on a project. For some reason, this individual rubbed me the wrong way. At the time – and I did not realize this - my default mind was in the driver's seat.

Without any basis in the current reality, I summarily dismissed him, always coming away from our interactions with a feeling of annoyance bordering on aggravation.

After rejecting his second overture to work together and feeling the same level of agitation, I paused and asked myself, why does this individual bother me so much? I have never had a bad experience with him in the past. He is someone who is in high regard in our industry. What is it about him that I do not like? And then it hit me.

When I was young, I spent a good deal of time with a friend who was smooth as silk from the standpoint of getting us into trouble but always managed to talk himself out of it. Unfortunately, I was often left holding the bag of responsibility for his actions. I felt angry, used, and betrayed and rightfully so. Now here is the power of the default mind; this individual in the present bore a strong resemblance to that friend. I would not suggest that they were twins, but the physical characteristics and their mannerisms were very similar.

Because I had been burnt in the past by my friend, my default mind, engaging the fight or flight mechanism (in this case flight) sought safety in the present solely on the resemblance between someone I had known decades earlier and someone in my present world. Remember, a default mind is an amazing tool that retains everything in order to keep you safe. It is when it runs unchecked and unchallenged, that it can negatively impact your present world.

In later chapters, I will talk more about critical thinking, including how Intentional Critical Thinking and Direct Experiencing work together to provide both a granular and big-picture perspective that can help you to recognize and manage your default mind. I will also go into greater detail of how these different yet complementary forms promote the insight required to accurately assess a present situation enabling you to take the necessary steps to either solve a problem or capitalize on a promising opportunity.

VUCA, an acronym developed during the Cold War to describe a social environment of Volatility, Uncertainty, Complexity and Ambiguity, is now in common use to describe our changing business world. It is important to understand in a VUCA world it is essential for your ongoing success and relevancy that you *recognize* that your old mind exists, and is driven by repetition, familiarity, and safety. It is also critical for you to understand that you must consciously make room for a new and complementary way of thinking, being, and ultimately doing. In other words, you need a new mind that can tap into your habitual thought process and intentionally leverage "what you already know" without it inhibiting or limiting "what you need to know" in the here and now.

The Purpose of This Book

Have you ever been so fixated on solving a problem that you can't seem to see the forest for the trees? Of course, you have. Everyone has to various degrees at one point or another. It is at those times of intense heat when you are "locked-in" and "zeroing in" on a challenging situation, your vision narrows to the point that you cannot see or hear anything beyond your problem zone. It is in this zone that the old mind's autopilot kicks in and you revert to a familiar pattern of response based not on what the present situation requires, but what your conditioning and training have taught your mind to see. At that moment, you stop asking questions and stop seeking greater understanding. Instead, you move to the pre-programmed response, i.e., knee-jerk mode, where there is a greater chance that you will not make the right decisions when facing a new or variable situation that extends beyond your expectations and experiences.

The purpose of this book is to give you the tools to access and more intentionally utilize past experiences and learnings without it obfuscating your ability to see, be, and act in the present where your attention is most needed.

I will also take you beyond the "fight or flight" mechanism showing you how to step back from an intense situation so that you can activate the new mind and empower yourself to own the situation rather than it owning you.

Finally, I will lay down the groundwork for establishing a new level of mindfulness that will propel you towards greater success by opening the door to increased mental agility and adaptive capabilities.

Within this context, you need to understand and reconcile the following:

1. Your default state of mind or auto-pilot thinking is operational under the radar throughout most of your waking life. In other words, and unless your mind is snapped out of this state by an exceptional event such as a beautiful sunrise or sunset, or shock moment such as narrowly avoiding an accident while driving, you live for the most part inside your head. Call it an endless loop of self-fulfilling judgments and repeat performances that project your past experiences and beliefs on the world around you.

2. You may be one of those individuals who feel that you work best under pressure, such as by a looming deadline, or a threat to your relationship with a client or co-worker. Only then, can you rise to the challenge and succeed. So, what is wrong with rising to the challenge? Let's face it we all admire a rags to riches story where someone goes beyond their apparent limitations to achieve a "little engine that could" outcome against all the odds.

The problem is that once the crisis has passed, you revert to the default state, meaning that your achieving potential is not originating within yourself but is driven predominantly by external forces. Why let circumstances determine your success? Why accept mediocrity - or the equivalent of mediocrity - given your performance under pressure, when you have the capability for consistent and continuous excellence? Ask yourself what is reverting to and living in your default state costing you?

Given the above, the best way to sum up the purpose of this book is to wake you up from your "sleep-walking" state to a conscious state where you live and achieve and realize your true potential in a present world.

SECTION I
UNDERSTANDING YOUR MIND

CHAPTER 1

THE MIND AS MASTER

"Life is 10% of what happens, and 90% of how (we) react to it."

- Charles Swindoll

Change is inevitable. Circumstances that happen beyond your control are almost a given, as the uncertainty and complexity of a dynamic world that is in constant motion intrude like an unexpected guest on your daily life.

In times of volatility, uncertainty, complexity, and ambiguity (VUCA), your mind – I will call it the old or conditioned mind, with its pre-programmed narrative, can be as much of a hindrance as it is a benefit, especially when you attempt to confine and define external events to what you know or think you know versus what you should learn.

Guided by this internal narrative, you then make decisions.

The problem is that like a switch that automatically turns on without your being aware of it, the decisions you make may not represent the best response because you have not had the opportunity to take in new and relevant information. Or the "new" information you have chosen has been sifted through your old biases in which your default-mind narrative has "cherry-picked" what it perceives as meaningful and relevant information.

In other words, and as much as external forces can have a disruptive impact on your decision making and self confidence, it is your inner state or influences that can cause the most havoc. That's right, your mind is either your greatest ally or worst enemy depending on how it has been pre-programmed and how it uses that information. In this context, your mind makes a great servant but an awful master as the saying goes.

Awareness and Commitment

If knowledge is power, then self-knowledge is the ultimate force that can help you to transform your inner state of mind.

Often referred to as having emotional intelligence, true knowledge of oneself is when you recognize that circumstances, people and perhaps more notably sensory influences, are pushing your buttons, triggering an automatic response.

Sensory influences are notable because they can seemingly emerge out of nowhere without your being consciously aware of them. In this regard, our ordinary, everyday default mind accounts for much of how we feel and think in the present world and therefore, can create a great deal of angst.

For example, you are walking and the wafting aroma of fresh baking instantly takes your mind back 30 years to memories of your grandma and how she baked the best pies. Those were the good old days, you wishfully think, realizing just how much you miss her and wishing that you could tell her how much you appreciate all she did for you. You then begin to feel sad, even regret not telling her how much she meant to you. In this example, not a person or a circumstance but one of the six senses, smell, has unconsciously stirred your emotions and created your dilemma or upset. Again, no person or event in the present time triggers your current feeling but instead your senses and subsequent discursive thinking and time travelling to past.

But self-knowledge of your thoughts is only half the picture, you also need to intervene to interrupt your trained thought process to determine if what you already know is valid and helpful in a present situation. Even more importantly, you need to open your mind to new possibilities while having the courage to resist what you may believe is the right response. It is the difference between siding with a commitment to new thinking, being, and doing, or sliding into an appeasement of old thinking.

Now I am not suggesting that the default mind does not have its usefulness. In truth, our pre-programmed thinking and subsequent responses resulting from past experiences can save us from a great deal of pain. For example, as a child, I would only need to touch a hot element on a stove once to learn for all time that doing so again in the future would burn my hand and cause pain. I do not have to spend cycles to relearn this.

But what if, by burning my hand on the element, I decide to never turn on the stove. That doesn't make a whole lot of sense; however, it illustrates the safety motivation of the pre-programmed mind. At that point, you must take a step back and ask if there is a better way to avoid burning your hand, and of course, there is.

As stated earlier, the old mind is driven by repetition and familiarity and motivated to achieve safety and, because of this, you perceive situations in absolute terms on a reflexive level (safe vs. unsafe). You have a natural tendency to go with old thinking because you accept it as a fact that it will guarantee safety and security. But fact and truth are two very different things here.

It is a fact that if you put your hand on a hot element, you will burn it. However, it is not true that turning on the stove will result in you burning your hand again. And it is in this middle ground between turning on the heat and touching the element that self-awareness (awareness of our thought process and old beliefs) and new intentional thinking in real-time must take place. As a result, I can turn on the stove, cook on the stove, but I do not have to touch the element with my hand.

I know this is an overly simplistic example, but it illustrates the point that turning on the stove to heat the element is not what caused you to burn your hand. One does not automatically lead to the other. In short, the old mind is limited to past cause and effect experience.

I will delve into understanding the old mind in greater detail in the next chapter.

CHAPTER 2

UNDERSTANDING THE REACTIVE OLD MIND

An experience provides knowledge which leads to understanding, and from mindful application of that understanding, you gain wisdom.

People often confuse knowledge and wisdom, thinking that they are the same. They are not. Knowledge comes through opening yourself up to seeing things in a different light, i.e. new experiences leading to greater insight and understanding. Wisdom is what you do with that understanding or how effectively you apply it to a particular situation or problem.

For example, the experience of driving lessons creates knowledge of the driving process that your brain saves as an accessible memory to which your default mind can refer when you drive a vehicle. How you choose to use that knowledge to drive skilfully, is where wisdom comes into play.

Unfortunately, moving from knowledge to understanding to wisdom and ultimately, a resolution or desired outcome is not a natural progression because the process can get hijacked by the old mind.

As a result, you need to train or retrain your mind to see things anew. Let's once again refer to the driving example. Your knowledge regarding how to drive must be complemented by moment to moment awareness to recognize changing road conditions and making the necessary adjustments in the here and now to ensure a safe trip. In the next chapter, I will provide you with an exercise using a simple glass of water that will help you to train your mind through experiencing rediscovery and expansion.

In the meantime, in this chapter, I want to provide you with the knowledge to understand how your old mind works. Through this understanding, you will come to realize that there is not a single decision or moment in your life that your mind is not influencing and impacting your choices, actions and outcomes either consciously or unconsciously.

Having this understanding, you will come to realize that the results you experience are not a mere coincidence but are the direct result of the quality of your mind's participation. When you realize that through cause and effect, your old mind is governing your response and decision-making behavior, you begin to take control of your life. When I say control of your life, I am talking about control of the source from which your responses originate.

Self-Awareness

What does it mean to say that someone is self-aware?

While self-awareness usually means being cognizant of your thoughts, feelings and physical sensations in the real time as they are taking place, when you become self-aware, you also become a witness to your experiences and how your mind responds or reacts in a given circumstance. It is as if you are taking a step back and objectively assessing a situation. This includes the level of interference from your default analytical/critical mind with its either insatiable fault-finding appetite that instinctively looks for what is wrong or missing. This will lead to thoughts of doubt 'what if I can't fix it?' and subsequently results in a feeling of fear and the physical sensation of contraction in legs and arms.

When you see things through a lens of objectivity, you recognize when you are bringing a judgemental mindset to the table and manage it so that it does not hijack your thought process. This ability to discern and manage the default analytical/critical mind is the beginning of wisdom. It means that you are becoming open to the possibilities of a new or different reality that empowers greater agility and creativity. As a result, there is enablement for you to move beyond the default impulse, to transforming it. It is thanks to this ability for transformation that true breakthroughs and resolutions ultimately come about.

CHAPTER 3
THE DAWN OF THE AGILE NEW MIND

As discussed in the previous chapter, self-awareness, which is the recognition of thoughts, emotions, and sensations in real-time, allows objectivity into your thought process – particularly when it comes to your emotional state. Specifically, self-awareness allows for observation & self-management allows for the interruption of the old or default mind's pre-programmed mechanism. Through this interruption, you either modify or transform your reaction to the corresponding default emotions of fear, anxiety, and anger, which can act like weeds choking out any creative agile response if you remain in an unaware state.

Of course, I am not suggesting that emotions are inherently bad. They are not. The problem with strong emotions that are triggered by the default habitual mind is that you lose the ability to learn about them and how to decipher their message/intelligence because you are busy reacting to them as opposed to witnessing and understanding (or inner-standing) them objectively, emotionally, and physically. It is when you step outside of yourself and the intensity of a situation, and enter a state in which you no longer judge emotions as being either good or bad that you gain emotional intelligence and the power to act in a manner that will lead to the best outcome.

For the sake of greater clarification, here are the differences between understanding and intentional inner-standing.

Understanding is useful and necessary, but it is still at the level of theory in the head. Inner-standing is stepping into your emotion by consciously and attentively, embodying it with a higher level of awareness and in the absence of judgment. Because of this element of judgment, you can be momentarily and fully aware that you are angry, but that understanding is immediately "covered" by old mind's knee-jerk judging thereby limiting it to being either good or bad, i.e., "my anger is either justified or unjustified." Conversely, with inner-standing, you can step into your emotions with a curious mind instead of a judgemental mind and are better able to see and experience the emotion in a broader and more revealing context. As a result, you gain additional insight and intuition such as what thought preceded the emotions, or what triggered the way I feel – remember the story of my friend and the impact my experience with him had on my present-day relationship with another individual? Gaining this insight will provide you with greater wisdom to unlock the intelligence in the emotions to achieve a beneficial result or outcome. As I stated at the beginning of this chapter, emotions are not inherently bad. Through inner-standing, they serve a valuable purpose when properly applied to real-world circumstances.

Witnessing & Direct Experiencing – A New Way Of Learning

I'd like to share with you an exercise developed by Jon_Kabat Zinn for *Mindfullness Based Stress Management Workshops*. You'll need to get a glass of water. I'll wait for you before we start.

Let's imagine for a moment that you are from another planet and that you have never experienced water before. Now look at the item in the cup and examine its qualities, what do you observe?

You may rightfully say that it is clear and takes the form of the cup. There is no smell to it.

Now close your eyes and take a sip. What is your experience with it? How does it taste? How does it feel as it hits your tongue? What did you feel when it was in your mouth? Was it refreshing?

Was there a sound when you drank the water? What was your natural impulse when you first took a sip?

When you were drinking the water, what were you thinking? Did you judge your experience when you took a sip or were you open to experiencing it?

While you have likely had thousands of glasses of water over your lifetime, most likely when you were fully present "in the moment," you became more aware of the water's properties right at the time without judging them as either good or bad. In the absence of thinking or judging in a default state, you were empowered to be in the moment and experience the water in a new way.

Being in the moment is what happens when you momentarily suspend habitual ways of perceiving something or someone with corresponding judgments, and instead provides you with the freedom to experience a situation directly and fully. It is through this unfiltered and unencumbered direct experience that you gain the knowledge that leads to greater insight and intuition, resulting in the wisdom to take meaningful and productive action.

You are, in essence, renewing your mind and with it your ability to consider alternative responses or solutions to a situation that would not have otherwise been available to you previously. Think of it in terms of upgrading your system's Windows software to a newer more relevant, and capable version. It is in this same way, we are upgrading our mind with the ability to handle more complexity in a VUCA world. In essence, you are no longer trying to address your pre-programmed analytical old mind's definition of reality, but instead the updated reality of the present moment.

Another way to put it, is that when you step outside of your old way of thinking you are no longer trying to prove what you know but are now discovering what you need to know in the here and now, moment by moment. At this point, you have activated the new present mind, as opposed to reacting to the old or reactive analytical mind.

And it is with this understanding of how the new mind works that I will, in Section II, introduce you to the 9-Steps for developing inner leadership for a changing world.

SECTION II
NINE STEPS TO AN AGILE MIND, OPEN HEART

CHAPTER 4
THE TOOLS FOR TRANSFORMATION

Physicist Albert Einstein often quoted as saying, "We can't solve problems by using the same kind of thinking we used when we created them." However, this is exactly how the default mind is programmed. Within split seconds, and beyond your awareness, default thinking feeds into and hijacks your conscious mind. As a result, you view real world situations through a judgemental lens that creates a reactionary cascade of associative thoughts and feelings that does not usually align to reality.

What is an example of the default thinking that feeds into the default mind creating this misperception and reality disconnect?

A client recently recounted his experiences while walking through a store parking lot.

Having just exited his car and in making his way to the store, an older woman driving a truck turned the corner and instead of stopping to let him pass, zipped by without any notice that he was there.

In seeing her face behind the wheel, within an instant, his default thoughts led to the conclusion that the woman was inconsiderate and crotchety. This judgemental and critical thinking triggered his default mind to role-play through countless negative scenarios, including the type of exchange of words he would have with the woman. With each cycle through the various scenarios of confrontation and continuing assumption of the older woman's thoughts and motives, he found his level of agitation steadily increasing. It was at this point, and through having self-awareness - which is Step 1 in the 9-Step process I will be introducing in the next chapter - he interrupted his imaginary narrative which was escalating his angst and irritability.

He then looked at the situation through a different mindset intentionally and the acknowledgment that he may not know the facts regarding why the woman did not notice him. Perhaps she had just received a troubling call or was distracted because she was on her way to visit a sick friend. The moment he stopped and changed his perception of the situation, his mind became open to other possibilities than her being thoughtless and inconsiderate. He was then able to introduce empathy into the equation, which ultimately diffused his negative emotions.

Triggered by default thinking which is the result of past experiences, i.e. the assumption that someone who does not cede the way to a pedestrian is rude and dismissive, the default mind instinctively, and in the absence of reasoning, looks for problems and, more specifically, the negative in any situation. The reason for this is that the default mind, yours and mine, views and assesses what happens in the world from the standpoint of an instantaneous thought process that compares, judges, criticizes, generalizes, all within a split of a second without the benefit of a due process. Hardly the basis for rational assessment and solution discovery.

Even worse, this is a normal modus operandi for the majority of humanity, if not all of the time, at least much of the time. Think about that for a moment. When we are operating out of this mode whereby instinctively the fight or flight habitual mind, which seeks safety above all else, is at the control of our thought process you can see why there are tension and conflict in our daily lives. Since we are living in a VUCA world, where security and certainty do not exist, there is a further magnification of this reaction. It is almost as if we are, to varying degrees, reaction-driven ping pong balls smashing against each other in response to a force that by its very nature is both impulsive and lacking in wisdom. It is because of the default mind's reactive process that self-awareness is critical to training or retraining your mind and heart.

It is important to bear in mind that as our self-awareness and ability to stand back from a situation to view it through a more discerning and empathic eye increases, so too does the possibility of self-condemnation by the default mind.

Let me give you another example of how quickly the default mind can kick into action a second time.

In Your Mind's Sight-lines

Recently, I was standing in line to pick up a few bottles of water before returning to a group coaching session I was leading. Even though I had given myself plenty of time to return, the people in front of me were indecisive when they reached the checkout counter. Taking what my default mind saw as an unnecessary amount of time to decide what they wanted to purchase, I became impatient, even annoyed with them. Remember, the default mind is motivated to maintain safety above all, and therefore is "driven" by the perception of a threat, or problems.

As a result, and as was the case with the client in the parking lot, within a split second, I saw their behavior as slowing me down or perhaps even stealing my valuable time. After all, they should have known what they wanted to purchase before they got into the checkout line. Again, if you are not aware of how your default mind works, your inclination may be to say something or fume beneath your breath at how idiotic and insensitive these people can be by holding up a line.

From there and resulting from that fraction of a second of default thinking, your level of frustration can take root and rapidly multiply as the stress hormones, cortisol and adrenalin, are released. Once this chemical reaction occurs and enters your system, it can take a while to leave your body, which is why there is a carry-over effect well after the original incident has taken place. Besides the negative health implications, the cortisol can put a damper on your overall sense of well-being and can negatively impact your interactions with others after the fact. In short, it colors your entire world and can prejudice your perceptions of any event or person triggering a similar response within their mind as well – hence the earlier ping pong ball reference.

Such responses are not intentional but are the result of thousands of years of programming. Remember, the default mind is driven by actively looking for and instantaneously responding to situations in which there is a perceived threat or problem. For this reason, and through your self-awareness, you can prevent your default mind from hijacking your present here and now mind. What I am referring to is the activation of your intentional or aware mind to manage your default mind and harness its process to work for you rather than against you.

Ironically, it is at this point of awakening or self-awareness that many people drop out of the 9-Step program.

Let's return to my checkout line to find out why.

As I had stated earlier, I was becoming annoyed with the slowness of the people in front of me. Without training, my mind would have continued down the path of carrying that annoyance well beyond the incident itself. But, having committed to activating my self-awareness and the corresponding self-management process, I was more prepared to recognize the default thinking in this instance and the subsequent default mind response. I could then intervene to diffuse the chain of reactive emotions and properly view and respond to what is happening in the here and now. There is just one problem; the default mind, which is always judging and critiquing, interrupts my intervention with self-condemnation in the form of saying, "Look at you, what kind of executive coach are you? You have been a coach for so many years, yet you still reacted the way that you did!"

To put it more succinctly, because the program is successful regarding the creation of a new self-awareness or mindfulness, you will step into your default mind's line of sight.

For some, having their default mind turn its attention from an external third party towards themselves is very difficult. Rather than seeking greater self-awareness, they decide to leave the program. Unfortunately, they continue down the path of oblivious reaction with all of its unintended consequences.

For this reason, and referring to my checkout line story, the following 3-step process developed by Kelly McGonigal in her program *The Neuroscience of Change,* is extremely helpful.

Disarming Your Default Mind

- Step 1 – I tell myself, "Kam, I can see you are thinking that after years of experience as a coach, you are still being hijacked and upset by your reaction in the line.

- Step 2 – You know that what is happening to you happens to everyone, including your mentors in the past. In short, what you are experiencing is not unique to you. Everyone experiences what you did.

- Step 3 – I want to honor you as well as commend you for your growing self-awareness in recognizing your reactions in the first place. Well done!

Did you see what I did there? I changed the narrative in my head from the judgemental default mind to the present, self-aware mind.

By doing so, I was freeing myself to see and assess things appropriately in the here and now without the backlash of self-condemnation and it is at this point that the incident ended with no carryover to my next interactions. The reason is simple, and as illustrated in the chart below, my intentional, self-aware mind is "not driven" by fears, threats, or problems. My intentional mind is "driven" by values, purpose, vision, and service, of which wisdom and patience are two attributes.

Default/Habitual State of Mind	Intentional/Aware State of Mind
Dominated by memory	Characterized by moment-to-moment present awareness
Values safety and control above all	Values meaning and curiosity
Driven by fear, problems & threats	Driven by purpose and vision
Hijacked by thoughts & strong emotions	Aware of thoughts and emotions
Acts and decides impulsively	Applies wisdom and discernment
Impatient	Patient
Exclusive and narrow worldview (mostly concerned with self)	Expansive and inclusive worldview (attentive to well-being of others)

Now that I have provided you with the framework of how both the default and intentional minds work, you are now ready for learning about the 9-Steps to put and keep control of your life where it belongs with your intentional and self-aware mind.

CHAPTER 5

THE 9-STEPS

After reading Chapter 4, hopefully, you came away with a good understanding of how the default mind can override your conscious or intentional mind and derail your thinking in the here and now. I also hope that you see how the inability to recognize and ultimately manage your default mind can lead to negative consequences for both yourself as well as others. Our purpose is to learn to manage the default mind so it becomes an asset instead of a liability.

Now you may be wondering at this point, why does my mind work this way? Is it somehow broken? Do I have a major character flaw in which my "wrong thinking" sends me down the slippery slope of unwarranted fears and unjustified anger?

To start, you do not have a character flaw, and no, your mind is not "broken." Truthfully, the way your default mind works is an example of just how amazing the mind is. In past times, when real dangers - like being eaten by a predator was a distinct possibility of everyday life - the default mind's ability to instantly assess and respond appropriately to threats is what kept our ancestors alive. Of course, as civilization progressed, the traditional and inherent dangers that once posed a serious threat began to disappear, but the default mind remained timelessly the same.

Perhaps this is why TV shows like *Survivor* are so popular today because our default minds thrive in such hostile environments where a wrong move may not get you eaten, but it will get your torch extinguished along with a boat ride home.

In other words, with *Survivor*, as contrived as it may be, threat and danger are imminent and real because at any time your life on the island can come to an end.

A New Mind For A New Time

Even though the threats and dangers of today's VUCA world can be daunting and upsetting, the type of response that is needed is not the same as in the distant past. As a result, the default mind, as it has traditionally worked, will not keep us safe today if left unchecked and managed via a collaborative interaction involving our intentional or conscious mind. Quite the opposite as it will cause us more harm than good if left to its own unchecked devices. Therefore, we need to train ourselves to activate our reliance on our intentional or "awake" mind using its attributes such as wisdom and patience to discern and leverage the default mind's input effectively. To be clear, I am not talking about dispensing with your default mind or bring it to an end, as much as I am talking about how we interact with it and ideally make friends with it so that we can learn its ways and utilize its input more effectively when appropriate.

In this context, think of this training or "retraining" of the mind as updating your internal thought software, i.e., Mind 4.0. The following introduction to the 9-Steps is an overview of your upgrade path.

STEP #1

INNER SELF-OBSERVATION

"Successful leadership depends on the quality of attention and intention that the leader brings to any situation. Two leaders in the same circumstances doing the same thing can bring about completely different outcomes, depending on the inner place from which each operates."

- Claus Otto Scharmer

While the inherent traits regarding how the default mind and the intentional mind work are consistent for all humans, the way we respond to external stimuli or events will be different depending on our unique individual life circumstances and experiences.

When facing common dangers, such as being robbed at gunpoint or suddenly having to swerve your car to avoid an accident, will trigger more or less the same default fight or flight chain reaction, our response to less dramatic or acute everyday events can be vastly different.

For example, despite my response to the long wait at the checkout counter, the person in front of me would likely have had an entirely different reaction based on their unique life experience. The reason for this is very simple; there are common biological and universally accepted extreme and life-threatening circumstances such as coming face to face with a rattlesnake on a hike will elicit the same reaction in just about everybody. However, in normal or everyday interactions, such as standing in line or being cut off in the parking lot, there is a more subjective reading and mental adding-on element to whether we perceive this as either good or bad which can originate back as our early childhood years.

The simple analogy of whether one sees a glass as being either half-empty or half-full best illustrates this last point. If you are of the half-empty mind, you are likely going to view the situation from the standpoint of an unfulfilled want or need that requires immediate action. In essence, it is "what is missing" or a "lacking" perspective or judgment. If you are a half-full person, you are more than likely going to see an exciting and great opportunity to add more to the glass. In other words, it will be a "what is already present" or "working" perception that will govern your subsequent response and course of action.

As an aside, and without overthinking the glass analogy, you may say, either way; the glass will be "refilled" to the top. That may be true, but the attitude and mindset through which you arrive at that end-result will be different, as well as its effect on yourself and others. To put it another way, a dysfunctional, *half-empty* team may achieve its goals or objectives, but the price that is paid to do so ultimately undermines the process and experience and therefore is not a sustainable model. A reflection and even verification of this latter point is the ever-increasing frequency in which people experience burnout. With its surge of adrenaline and cortisol, when you are constantly operating in fight or flight mode (from a negative standpoint), it is like continuing to rev your car's engine at the maximum RPM rate. Eventually and much sooner than operating your vehicle at a reasonably sustainable RPM rate, your car will break down. Common in leadership situations, this "revving" can show itself in the form of you being an "overly driven," go-it-alone leader who fails to create a shared vision with your team. By excluding your team and relegating them to the role of spectators means that your efforts will only have short-term success at the ultimate expense of long-term sustainable productivity.

The bottom line is that your perceptions and subsequent reactions to life events will be different from someone else. As a result, you want to become self-observant of how *your mind* works so that you can consciously recognize when and how the default mind is being "triggered." You can then intervene with your intentional, conscious mind to ensure that there is an appropriate response based on your deepest intentions as well as an accurate perception of facts in the here and now.

In the above example, regarding the go-it-alone leader, becoming self-observant means that you recognize what is commonly known as the heroic impulse to save the day by single-handedly charging up the hill alone. Being aware of the impulse is Step #1. Learning how to manage this impulse skilfully is Step #2.

STEP #2

INNER SELF-MANAGEMENT

"Fear is the cheapest room in the house; I'd like to see you in better living conditions." -Hafiz of Persia, Sufi theosopher

Knowing oneself and taking action on that knowledge are two very different things. Therefore one of the biggest challenges you will face is to step outside of yourself in order to look beyond your impulsive reactions to situations and harness that energy into a skilful as opposed to debilitating action.

To do this, you must move beyond merely reacting to how your default mind works. Instead, you have to make a conscious effort not only to recognize and be aware of the initial impulse but also to interrupt the pre-programmed mind and introduce a new way of thinking, being, or doing that reflects your values, intentions, and the reality of the here and now instead of the experiences of yesterday and the fears of the future. With this second step, I will show you how to interrupt and manage the old impulsive habits.

Overcoming "What If...?"

One of the most famous sayings is the one by Mark Twain, who said that "I have had a lot of worries in my life most of which never happened."

Fear, and "what if...?" scenarios, can produce feelings of discomfort and uneasiness. The key is understanding the differences.

You are walking down the street and out from behind a house, a big dog charges towards you. What is your reaction? If you do not know the dog and it is barking, are you afraid or somewhat wary? This response is what is known as biological fear. It is instinctual and similar to your response when you suddenly have to swerve your car to avoid an accident to be safe. During such events, you are in the present moment.

Let's look at a different scenario.

It is late, and you are tossing and turning in bed, finding it unable to sleep. Why can't you sleep? Maybe you have an upcoming big presentation to give in front of a large audience or had a meeting earlier in the day that did not go well, and you are cooking up imaginary consequences in your head. This kind of "time-traveling" fear is psychological and has more to do with thinking and thoughts and images generated in your head than an actual angry client or barking dog in your bedroom where there is no imminent danger.

In a situation like this, one of two things happen; you allow your default mind to hijack you as you "time travel" between past experiences - usually negative recollections- and future imaginations – usually worst-case scenarios.

Alternatively, you can try to either deny or ignore your fears or distract yourself by turning to food or drink. Of course, anything you resist will persist and perhaps become more acute. Distraction only numbs the underlying default thinking causing the fear which will afterward return with greater intensity because you have hidden from it instead of dealing with it.

The Battle Within

Once again, and similar to biological fear, psychological fear originating in the default mind occurs within milliseconds and out of the realms of the conscious mind. At this point, you can allow your default mind to race ahead of you unchallenged, you can try to wrestle control of your thoughts away from the default mind through the various distractions to which I referred above. Alternatively, you can assume a state of Meta-Cognition/Meta-Awareness, or what J. Krishnamurti calls "Choiceless Awareness" is the ultimate solution to the reactive default mind. It is a higher state of mind – an awareness of awareness itself, that enables you to observe your reactions without making any effort or choice to heed the story or fear scenarios being played out by the default mind. In essence, it is stepping out of yourself to become a witness to your reactions and thereby becoming grounded as a neutral observer.

So, and in the context of the above, when you find yourself in the center of an emotional storm, seemingly held prisoner by swirling thoughts that you cannot contain. What can you do?

You have the following three options.

1. You can remain in a reactive state employing various distractions which will provide at best momentary relief but will inevitably bring you back to the same place.

2. You can use various "techniques" to manage the strong emotions/impulse without being swept by their pull.

3. You can shift to a higher state – a choiceless awareness state that educates the mind about its reactive habits and

thus upgrades your mind to a more effective version of itself.

I will provide a more detailed explanation of how to train your mind to get to this higher state of Choiceless Awareness in the "Interrupting The Cycle" section. It's important to know when you allow the mind to run its course and use up its energy regarding a fearful thought or thoughts you come to a resting place.

What do I mean by resting place?

Think of a glass of water and mud. When you stir the contents of the glass, which represents your mind the swirling water and mud obfuscate your ability to see the contents clearly. However, when you stop stirring and set the glass down what happens? The mud will soon settle at the bottom, and you will have a clear view, i.e. a clear mind.

When you apply Choiceless Awareness, you see more at a much deeper level. You learn how your mind works as the full thought cycle reveals itself and are thus able to self-manage by remaining an observer to the flow of the thoughts and emotions without getting caught by it.

Here is one example of how Choiceless Awareness enables

you to "witness/observe" your default mind's reactions to emotion of fear at a much deeper level.

1. The default mind attaches a label to your experience, "Fear is here!"

2. It then immediately personalizes the feeling, "I am afraid!"

3. It then passes the judgment; "This is bad!"

4. Next, default storytelling habit both exaggerates and catastrophizes the fearful scenario, compounding the intensity of fear, "I will always be afraid!"

5. Then there is the activation of the fight or flight mechanism and the corresponding release of stress hormones that lead to contractions in major muscles in the body. The contractions and discomfort trigger an immediate desire or impulse to end it and be free of it. The mind says, "I should not be afraid," "I should be brave, courageous" resulting in a crippling polarity between being "fearful" and wanting to be "courageous."

6. The crippling polarity or duality creates an internal conflict between mind's wanting to be courageous, yet having to contend with doubts regarding its own ability to achieve it. The mind then wants to solve the above

impasse by suggesting you flee to a distraction to ease the pressure of inner-conflict, i.e. call a friend, turn-on TV, grab a slice of cheesecake from the fridge (the 3rd slice of the day) go shopping or any other activity to help you get "away."

7. Since these activities are distractions and don't address the root problem, a part of you may know you will inevitably have to face yourself again in a similar situation. In other words, you will find yourself right back from where you started, at which point the default mind may self-judge resulting in the self-sabotaging narrative in which it thinks; "I am not good," and "There must be something wrong with me."

This is a crucial moment, if by now you have successfully continued to maintain an observing posture, having depleted its own energy the busy mind will collapse on itself and a moment of clarity will emerge - just like the mud that settles at the bottom of the glass if we simply avoid stirring it.

Since there will be moments that is not be possible or feasible to apply Choiceless Awareness, it will be more appropriate to attempt to manage and interrupt the strong emotions cycle, I offer the following strategies.

Interrupting The Cycle

Now that you have recognized at least some of the characteristics of how your default or habitual mind works when confronted with psychological fear, you can choose to train your conscious mind to interrupt the negative thought cycle.

Immediately upon becoming aware of your impulse to react to the intrusion of your default mind be it originating in fear or otherwise, you must make a conscious effort to choose to manage your reaction at either a physical, emotional or mental level or any combinations thereof.

Simple Physical Level Intervention

Generally, it is much easier to start with managing strong emotions by using your body/physical cues and sensations first, then emotions, and finally at thought level.

For example, your response to a difficult situation often shows up in one part of the body in the form of contraction when a feeling of worry or anxiousness first emerges. Let's say you think of tomorrow's meeting and anxious thoughts manifest as butterflies in the stomach. While most people may not be consciously aware of what is happening at an emotional level, i.e. the feeling of worry or anxiousness, they are often aware of having a "funny feeling in the stomach."

Therefore, self-management at the physical level may involve the simple act of scanning your body for any tightening or contractions and directing your breathing to the affected area. Guiding your conscious breathing to the affected area will manage the difficult emotions at the physical body level. While you are consciously guiding your breath to the affected area, you stop the rumination process as you cannot be simultaneously breathing with full awareness and also be feasting on worrisome thoughts. The two are mutually exclusive. Hence the relaxing impact. That is why breathing is such a universal remedy for an emotional hijack.

Emotional Level Intervention

What you name you tame. Simple noticing and naming emotions will often create greater awareness. For example, you can say "worry, worry," "anger, anger," "impatience, impatience" to identify your feelings at a given moment. Once you have established the awareness of the emotions, you can then use the conscious breathing and guide the breath to the affected body areas. This technique is also very helpful to protect yourself in the presence of strong emotions emitted by people in power. Let's say you are in a team meeting, and the boss clearly shows signs of anger and frustration. If you are not "aware" within a split second you have already inherited his/her strong emotions through what neuro-scientists call "mirror neurons". However, if you silently label what emotions you observe in the boss, i.e., "anger, anger," "frustration, frustration," you can choose to self-manage and therefore avoid taking on their emotions.

Mind Level Intervention

In the moment of being triggered by a physical cue, becoming self-aware allows you to step back and enquire: What caused me to feel this way? What thoughts or images preceded how I am feeling? When else I felt the same…? It is at this point, as a witness to your emerging thoughts and emotions that you can choose to continue with inquiry or to stop all together.

On A Clear Day

A famous Alan Jay Lerner song claims, "That on a clear day, you can see forever." While the seeing forever part may be figurative, the fact is that when you experience your emotions through Choiceless Awareness, you step back from it and have a clearer perspective on what you are experiencing. In other words, when you avoid participating in ruminating or brooding and judging what you are experiencing as being either good or bad, you open yourself up to possibilities that you might otherwise not have considered.

You begin to operate in the present moment without

perceptions skewed by past experiences and future scenarios being played out via your highly imaginative default mind. You then enable your conscious in the moment mind to effectively take in more information and thus provide you with true context.

It is from this starting point that sound decision-making occurs because your perception regarding a given situation will be in alignment with reality. I will talk more about perception next, in Step #3.

STEP #3

ENHANCING PERCEPTION

"Seeing is not believing; believing is seeing! You see things, not as they are, but as you are."
- Eric Butterworth

Have you ever looked through a prism in which the refraction of a single light beam entering one side becomes many different colors on the other side?

The result of a phenomenon known as dispersion a prism demonstrates how a single perspective can express itself in many ways. In other words, we as individuals can all view the same situation, but for each of us, we will see it differently based on our unique past experiences.

As discussed in Steps #1 and #2, understanding that we have a unique view of circumstances or situations that are going to be different from others, and then managing ourselves with that understanding enables us to see things in a new light. In essence, we are changing the angle of the single light to reflect new colors and insights.

Let's revisit the barking dog scenario in the previous section.

You are walking down the street and a big dog charges towards you out from behind a house. What is your reaction? If you do not know the dog and it is barking, are you afraid or somewhat wary? Seeing the dog as a potential threat is your likely response. But what if the barking is not a sign of viciousness but playfulness? What if the dog is running towards you because he or she is friendly? What happens to you within those milliseconds between first seeing the dog and your reaction?

Your brain automatically assesses the situation, accesses like a high-speed computer your default mind memory banks looking for a relatable experience or belief from your past, and then signals to you that the situation you are facing is either dangerous or not.

Your first reaction is logically going to reflect your belief or what has happened to you in the past rather than what may be happening in the present.

For example, what if you grew up having had dogs for pets and when you came home from school every day they would come running towards you barking and happy to see you? What impact would this have on your response in our present scenario?

Conversely, if in your past experiences, a barking dog running towards you was associated with an unpleasant outcome, you are more likely to react defensively even if the said reaction is not warranted.

These differences are representative of the prism effect, i.e., the same single light coming in producing many different colors of light on the other side. Like the light exiting the prism, it is how we all perceive the same or similar situations differently that govern our choices and actions.

As Perceived So It Is Experienced

What is a perception? Perception is the way we see or interpret ourselves, others and the events around us. Furthermore, the way we perceive or interpret an event directly determines what we feel and how we act. If our perceptions are limiting or faulty to begin with, our course of actions will be flawed and we will not get the results or outcomes we wished for.

In the barking dog scenario, if you perceive that the dog's

actions are a threat, then your perspective or attitude will be defensive. However, if you perceive the dog's actions to be friendly, your attitude will be different and be reflected in your corresponding reaction or response.

For this reason, enhancing your perception and reframing your attitude will bring more truth into your life and therefore provide you with the ability to better respond to different situations through a more effective and productive lens.

Behind The Wheel: How Perceptions Influence Emotions

At this point, it is important to demonstrate that moving from being driven by default perception to a more robust perspective is not a destination but an ongoing journey. Achieving a continuous level of perspective that is in alignment with reality is not a static, one-time event, but one requiring the discipline to view a situation consciously beyond the initial perceptions that are triggered by the default mind. In short, we need to develop the right mind habits, something we will talk about in greater detail in step #4.

For example, I was recently driving on the Sheikh Zaid Road. For those familiar with Dubai, you will know that this is the longest highway in the United Arab Emirates. Running parallel to the coastline, it has multiple access points or on-ramps.

As I was entering the on-ramp to get on the highway, and being aware of needing to gain speed to enter the fast-moving lane safely, I found myself behind a slow-moving vehicle. When I honked my horn, the driver in front of me would speed-up slightly only to slow down again a few moments later. After honking, speeding-up, then slowing down a couple of more times, I became aggravated imagining different reasons for the driver's behavior such as their being incompetent or on the phone. As an aside, this on-ramp to the highway did not provide a passing lane, so I was "stuck" behind this driver. My perception was one that led to emotions of frustration and annoyance.

When I was finally able to get on the highway and pass the driver, I looked over and discovered that the man behind the wheel was elderly. Replacing my feelings of annoyance and agitation were feelings of understanding and empathy mixed in with a little self-recrimination.

The point is that once my perspective of the situation changed, my emotions and attitude automatically changed.

While my responsive thought process at the time brought me to a greater realization of the true nature of the situation in which I found myself, it does not mean that the next time I find myself in a similar circumstance, I will automatically recall this recent event and respond accordingly. In other words, for your perspective to be in continuous alignment with the real world, you must make a conscious effort to interrupt the default mind's existing perceptions, and ask yourself is what I am thinking based on current day facts or past perceptions.

It is worth noting at this point that the origin of my perception that the person driving the vehicle in front of me was either incompetent or distracted is likely the result of a "hidden belief." Dealing with hidden beliefs, which we will discuss in greater detail in Step #5, is an important part of moving from a default perception response to a real-world perspective through the introduction of new mind habits.

The focus of Step #3, is to move you from being driven solely and myopically by default internally driven perception, which does not always align with the reality before you, to a broader real-time perspective.

A Victim Of Past Success

We all know that our perceptions or view of the world is in large measure a result of our past experiences, such as with the barking dog. Because of this, our perspective of the world around us is not only skewed but significantly narrowed. It is this continuous narrowing through the recycling and reinforcement of past experiences that our reactions and behaviors become more ingrained and even more difficult to change. The reason for this "narrow mindedness" is not because there is an inability to learn, but rather because the old perceptions are so ingrained that they have become a belief. This obstacle is especially problematic in situations where past behavior has produced successful results or have proven to be true.

Let's revisit my experience behind the slow-moving driver.

If after seeing that there was an older person behind the wheel, I had the belief that someone that old should not be allowed to drive, I would have been justifying my feelings of annoyance and agitation. Instead of letting go, I might have continued to hang on to those feelings, perhaps even having them escalate which would have possibly come out in my meeting with the next person. So, rather than recognition and empathy, I would have instead felt justified and perhaps even superior for being supposedly "right."

Seeing yourself as being either right or wrong may be different paths, but they all lead to Rome in that they narrow your vision and ultimately your thinking and with it, your ability to effectively operate in the here-and-now world. That is why you should not view feelings and thoughts as being either right or wrong but seek to understand them. With the latter, you always maintain an open mind, while with the former, your mind gradually and progressively becomes closed. In this way, the lens of your perception becomes increasingly myopic, and therefore you lose the ability to have a meaningful perspective.

In business, countless companies fell into irrelevance because the perception of their past success narrowed their perspective to one of "we are always right because we have been right before" or, "we have always done it this way, why should we do it differently now."

The reason this "locked-in" thinking occurs is due to what scientists call ingrained neural patterns.

What You Think, You Become

Remember the exercise of experiencing a drink of water as if it were the first time even though it is the millionth time. To do this involves both the willingness and flexibility to reprogram your mind to ensure that you have a fresh perception of the experience.

When I talk about reprogramming your mind, I am referring to the process of challenging and if necessary, rerouting the ingrained neural patterns that operate habitually through the conscious moment-to-moment intentional experiencing.

As a leader in today's fast-moving VUCA world, this is

critical as you must be self-aware when it comes to how you think and what you think. This self-knowledge or awareness gives you the ability to identify patterns of thought that can adversely impact your decision-making process.

To begin the process that will lead to greater self-understanding and ultimately to breaking potential patterns of unproductive thinking, you must have flexibility.

So, what are the attributes of a flexible leader?

Benefits Of A New Pattern

As previously mentioned, there are countless stories of industry leaders who fell victim to past success and buying into the belief that being right in the past means that they are going to be right in the future and are, therefore, unwilling to change.

For example, at one time, Swiss watches were the watchmaking gold standard for excellence. In 1968, the Swiss had a 65% share of the global wristwatch market. What is worth noting, is that they rejected the home-grown invention of the Quartz watch, as it didn't match their perception and belief of how a watch should be made incorporating jewels, bearings, gears and springs.

Seiko and Texas Instruments did not share such sentiments

or perceptions and purchased the technology in 1968. Within couple of decades Swiss market share globally for watches had dropped to only 10%.

Their perception of what a watch should be, which had been "ingrained" for generations led to the perspective that ultimately proved to be inaccurate and out of touch with what the market wanted. Because of their erroneous beliefs, they failed to perceive the new realities and possibilities. They became the victim of their once helpful but now outmoded perception.

You will note that I used the words "perception" and "belief" interchangeably in the above story. There is a reason I did this. Many of our perceptions have been shaped over time, becoming unchallenged beliefs. The insistence by the Swiss watch industry that there was only one way to build a product is one example.

Another more universal example is how, as children, we are born with an inherent trust that everything our parents say or do is right.

At a young age, and as a matter of survival, we do not question a parent taking our hand and telling us to look both ways before crossing the street. But, beyond irrefutable examples such as looking both ways before stepping off the curb of the sidewalk, there are a great many subjective beliefs that are not universal and are therefore subject to scrutiny.

The challenge with being able to scrutinize said beliefs is that we usually establish them early in life through not only active witnessing but also by osmosis. Beliefs seep into our value system and once held to be true are difficult to identify because they have become second nature and hidden which makes them nearly impossible to surrender or even modify.

In Step #5, we will delve deeper into identifying and understanding your hidden beliefs, including their origins and their subsequent influence on the formation of your default mind affecting how you think and interact with the world around you.

But before we can get to that stage, you first need to have the proper "mind habit" tools to claim back the power invested in your default reactive mind. Achieving this makes identifying and changing limiting hidden beliefs easier.

STEP #4

MIND HABITS

> *"Security is a double-edged sword: While a fence sure protects the fenced; it also imprisons the protected."*
> – Mokokoma Mokhonoana

The default mind seeks security above all else. Because of its myopic focus on safety, the default mind offers false promises based on familiar and therefore, safe beliefs. The reason that it is a false promise is that in the desire to protect you by keeping you in a familiar and comfortable pattern of thinking it hijacks and imprisons your thought process to a habitual "safe" way of doing/being, thereby shutting out your ability to think intentionally, learn and grow. As a result, your actions are reactive rather than proactive because the decisions you make reflect what your default mind deems to be the truth when in actuality its assessment does not usually align with reality.

With Step #1, we explored how the default mind leads to default thinking and the limitations associated with it. In Step #2, we explored default emotions as the by-product of default thinking and how to recognize and manage them. In Step #3, we talked about how the default mind leads to default myopic perception. In Step #4, we will now establish the framework for instilling the proper mind habits starting with identifying default mind habits and how your current "habits of thinking" impact your life.

What Is The False Promise?

All mind habits begin with a promise that originates in the default mind.

When I talk about a false promise, I am referring to the apparent benefits of a way of thinking, doing, or being that on closer examination hinder rather than help.

Let's take a perfectionist mind habit as an example.

For many always striving to know and understand everything all the time or always demanding perfection from oneself as well as others is an attribute to be admired. The false promise perfectionism gives is that if you get an A+ on an exam, never miss a putt on the golf course, or always say and do the right thing, all will be well and you will be safe. The only problem is that perfection is a continuous journey or ongoing development as opposed to being a final destination. In short, you and all people, including myself, are a work in progress. To the perfectionist, this is an unacceptable state of compromise and even failure.

In the context of the above, let's consider the leaders who are perfectionists and attend my EQ & Self-Reflective group coaching sessions. They are almost always the first to feel agitation and frustration if they do not immediately understand every element of the program. As a result, their default mind goes from championing perfection to judging their inability to live up to standards that are, in reality, unattainable. This judgment, in turn, leads to a self-criticism that undermines confidence driving them to become more demanding of themselves and others. It is a vicious cycle that plays itself out in a variety of controlling and detrimental behaviors such as impatience, arrogance, or becoming overly critical. This response to falling short of expectations subsequently hurts relationships as the perception of the perfectionist leader is that others who do not live up to their standards are falling short as well.

There is no room for error with a perfectionist leader. Any

sign of imperfection even when warranted sounds their alarm siren as if their very life is at risk.

Everyone makes mistakes and misses the mark. Rather than castigation, acknowledging mistakes and looking for creative solutions to address them is the way to go. Such an approach illustrates perfectly the difference or point of disconnect between the default mind (perfectionism), and the conscious or intentional mind (solution & purpose-driven). However, with the perfectionist who operates through default rather than intentional thinking finding solutions takes a back seat to their seeking safety in the familiar confines of having full control through being perfect. Having total control beyond oneself and being perfect is, of course, an illusion and will surely lead to frustration for the leader and those around her/him sooner than later including conflict escalation, employee dissatisfaction, and higher turnover.

But does this mean that you should accept second best or not work towards operating at a higher level of performance? The answer is an unequivocal NO!

What it does mean is that instead of perfectionism being an automatic go-to habit, you must establish new "mind habits" that move perfectionism from the default judgemental mind to the intentional creative mind where there are an accurate perspective and context to transform it to an asset. I will talk about moving from reactive default thinking to creative, intentional thinking in the next section, including its impact on the perfectionist mind.

Addressing The Habit Void

Before I delve deeper into how, for example, perfection can become a positive asset, I want to explain why establishing new mind habits is critical to a sustainable transformation in the way you interact within yourself as well as with others externally.

When you recognize how your default mind works and take the appropriate measures to adjust your thinking process, you will inevitably create a temporary void. In other words, when you interrupt the habitual default process, you must replace it with something else. Otherwise, you are vulnerable to falling back into old patterns of thinking, perceiving, and behaving. However, to establish a new way of intentional thinking requires a cognitive and repetitive effort until it becomes second nature – a new default. Specifically, your default mind never goes away, nor should it because it still has an important role to play in everyday life. But, with the intervention of the intentional mind, you can identify, manage and reframe the default mind's message and make an informed decision based on new insights and understanding as opposed to impulse or old habits of perceiving and thinking.

For example, you are crossing the road and see a car coming

at you at high speed. You don't pause to wonder how fast is the car really going and whether it would manage to brake on time or who after all has the right of way you as a pedestrian or the speeding car. You respond by immediately getting out of the way. The default mind has served its purpose as it led you to safety.

Conversely, a client calls you to say they did not receive an anticipated shipment. Is your response one of panic, or upset, fretting over who to blame?

Without the intervention of the intentional mind, your blaming mind habit will get you trapped in unproductive impulsive reaction. In this loop you will waste cycles on everything from blaming yourself "Why didn't I handle the order through to delivery myself?" to judging others, and overgeneralizing and catastrophizing. "What is wrong with the people in shipping? They *always* mess things up; if this continues, we will lose *all* of our customers!" In extreme cases, you might even blame the client for having unreasonable expectations. In other words, and in its quest to protect and seek safety, the reactive default mind habits will judge, blame, over-generalize and catastrophize. It is at this point that the intentional mind must intervene by first recognizing and naming these limiting mind habits in order to neutralize their influence and then shifting the focus to accept what has happened and work collaboratively with the shipping department in a non-judgemental, non-blaming, non-catastrophizing way to find a resolution today and avoid a repeat in the future.

In the context of the errant shipment example, the following 360 Leadership Circle Profile™ graphic illustrates how managing reactive attributes such as perfection and autocratic mindsets (lower right half-circle) will through intentional interruption lead to the introduction of creative attributes such as collaboration, interpersonal intelligence, and team play (upper left half-circle). Filtering perfectionism or other default mind habits by identifying, naming and ultimately neutralizing the imbedded Hidden Beliefs that empower them (the topic of Step #5), we learn to transform these strongly embedded behaviors to creative attributes, that will foster better relations and lead to a more effective and timely resolution.

To better explain this graph, in the reactive lower hemisphere of the circle, the main dimensions are controlling, protecting and complying each of which operate in the realm of the default mind. With each dimension, there are associated behaviors. For example, controlling dimension includes perfectionist, driven, ambitious and autocratic behaviors. Without establishing the habit of intentional mind intervention, these behaviors when unchecked hinder relations in the creative upper hemisphere where the effective intentional leadership abilities reside. These intentional relating behaviors include caring connections, foster team play, collaborator, mentoring and developing, and interpersonal intelligence.

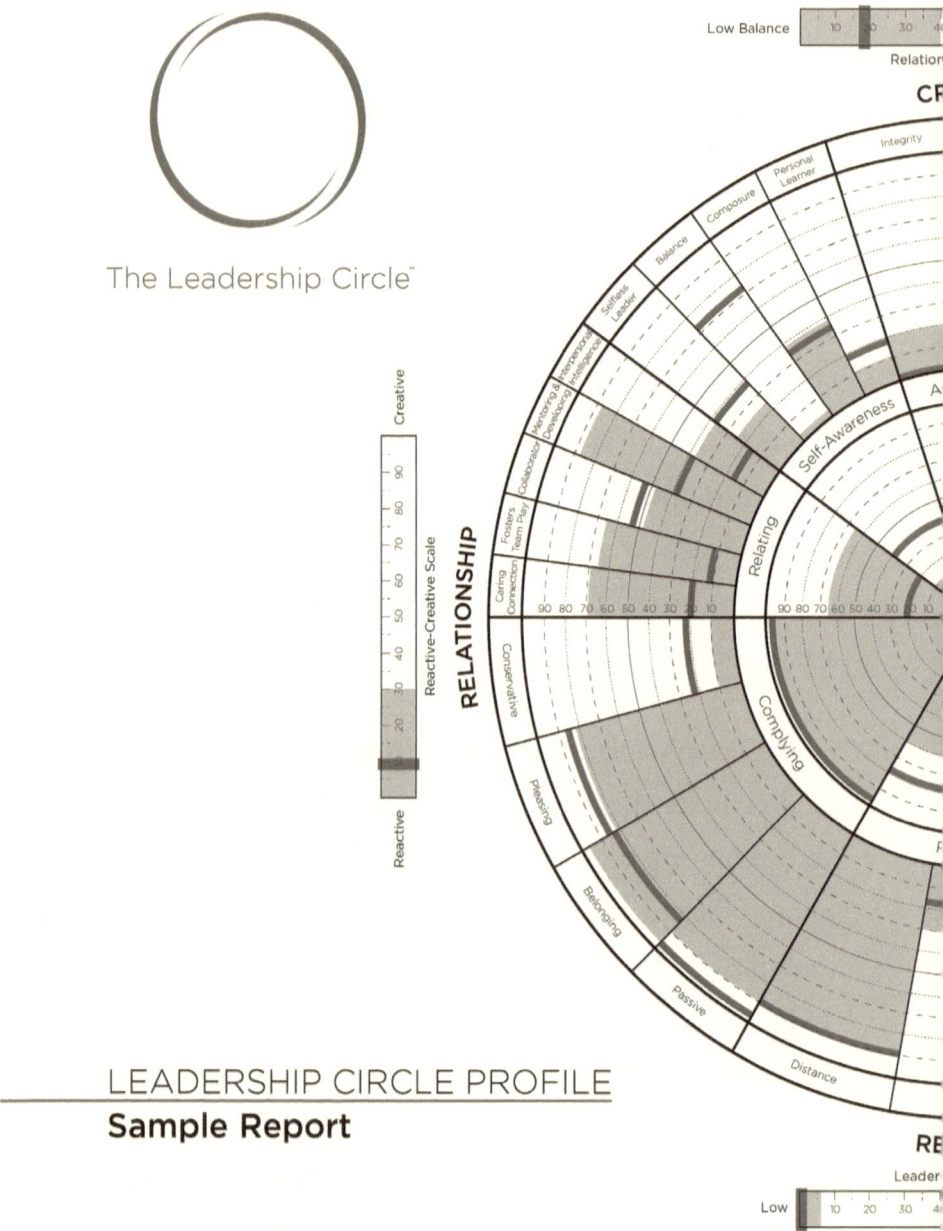

LEADERSHIP CIRCLE PROFILE
Sample Report

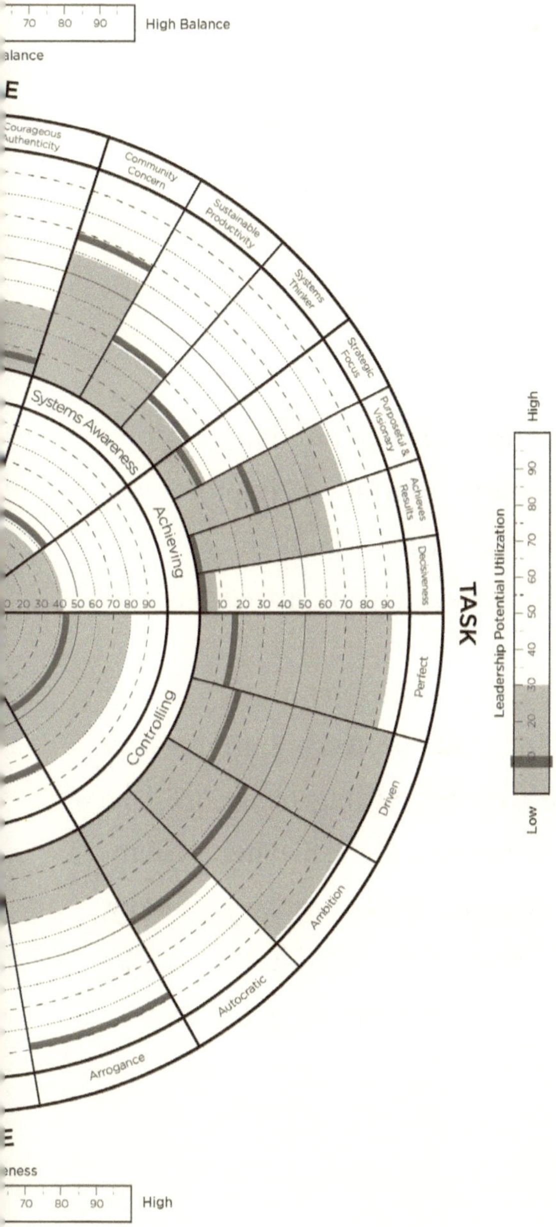

Agile Mind, Open Heart

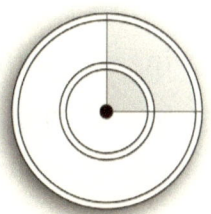

CIRCLE WITHIN A CIRCLE:

The inner circle profiles a percentile summary score for all dimensions in that section of the outer circle.

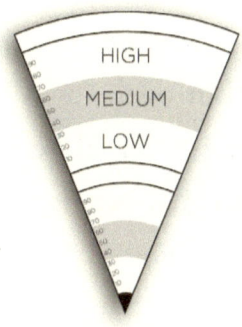

PERCENTILE SCORES:

High:
Scores from the 66th to the 100th percentile are strong scores.

Medium:
Scores between the 66th and the 33rd percentile show a mix of strength and areas of improvement.

Low:
Scores below the 33rd percentile are low scores.

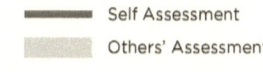

©The Leadership Circle® | All Rights Reserved

So, how does a perfectionist mind habit become beneficial when tempered with a creative, relational attribute? Specifically, it establishes a standard to ensure that the focus is always on achieving timely client deliveries. The perfect goal is a focus on "always" achieving timely delivery. But, the relational attributes which reflect behaviors such as collaborating, team building and learning recognize that an errant shipment is part of the process of doing business and therefore presents an opportunity to learn and improve.

Therefore, the mind habit is moving from reactive perfection within one's "own head" to one of continuous improvement using external relating and interacting which, it is worth noting, fosters leadership effectiveness and improved business performance.

Like controlling, complying, and protecting are reactive default mind dimensions with corresponding behaviors. The creative, intentional mind counterparts are achieving, systems awareness, authenticity and self-awareness respectively. The key, therefore, through the introduction of the mind habits exercise in the next section is to facilitate a move from reactive to creative dimensions.

Finding Your Balance

Recently, I was introduced to a client who despite having an IQ in the top 2%, was unable to get his career going. He was in a rut and could not get the necessary traction to move forward.

Because of the ongoing conflict with his coaches as well as others with whom he interacted, he could no longer find a coach who was willing to work with him. Within a short time after meeting him, he said; "I MUST get the next career *right*. I am already 35 and am so behind".

Can you spot or identify which default mind habits are operating behind his statement, and what default strong emotions would they generate?

Understanding the mind habits behind what someone is saying will ultimately provide insight into their default perception, why they do the things they do and provide the necessary insight to help them to transition from reactive default mind thinking and behaving to intentional creative mind thinking and behaving.

While the 35-year-old executive possessed a high IQ, he did not have the necessary emotional intelligence to help him understand his thinking and thus take control of his career path.

To better understand his challenges, let's examine more closely his statement, "I MUST get the next career *right*. I am already 35 and am so behind."

His insistence that he "Must get it *right*" is an indication that he is a Perfectionist in which he has absolutely no room for error. As a result, he is carrying a tremendous amount of self-imposed pressure, stress, and fear of failure with his unyielding "must get it *right*" belief and explained why he would not take action.

His lamentation that "I am already 35 and so behind" is both counter-productive and destructive in that he is comparing himself to others in his age category prompting thoughts of having fallen behind and defeated. Such thoughts of "not measuring up" triggers the self-criticism mind habit, i.e. "Everyone else my age is doing well, and I am not. What is wrong with me?"

Between the pressure of having to be perfect and a critical self-assessment of his supposed failure to live up to a perceived standard posed by the success of his peers, his default mind habits were getting him into a rut out that he could not escape.

The way for him to get out of the rut would be first to identify and then deal with his self-limiting default mind habits.

What default mind habits do you believe are limiting your ability to realize your full potential?

By going through the following exercise, you will learn how to identify limiting default mind habits and begin building a bridge between the isolation of your internal reactive default mind and your intentional creative mind. In other words, you will awaken your inner-awareness to identify the blind spots/limiting unseen assumptions (beliefs) that fire up your reactive mind habits and behaviors.

Scenario/Situation:

You leave the meeting and catch your default mind berating you: "I should not have said that. I should have said this or something else. I am such a fool!"

a) Name the default mind habits involved.

b) What subsequent default emotions/reactions do these generate?

c) What limiting hidden beliefs/unseen assumptions do you spot?

Getting To The Root

Have you ever weeded a garden? If you have, you know that if you only remove the visible leaves on the surface in a very short time, new leaves will appear. Therefore, the only way to remove the weed permanently is to dig it out at its root.

The same is true when it comes to identifying and debunking the hidden beliefs responsible for outdated mind habits.

In other words, making the transition from a mind habit such as perfectionism requires that you identify and neutralize the hidden belief that feeds it. By "digging it out," you will then be able to create a positive shift in your thinking and doing.

In Step #5, I will show you how to identify and neutralize the hidden beliefs that are undermining your ability to realize your full potential.

STEP #5

HIDDEN LIMITING BELIEFS

"A half-truth is even more dangerous than a lie. A lie, you can detect at some stage, but half a truth is sure to mislead you for long."

– Anurag Shourie

With Step #4, you gained the necessary insight into how your default mind habits impact your life and how through a few initial steps you can start to identify your blind spots and limiting unseen assumptions or beliefs and bring them into a collaborative alignment with your intentional mind.

Now that you have the tools to go through this process putting them into practice requires a good deal of commitment.

This because our belief system, which can be both factual but also subjective, and therefore non-factual, is a big part of who we are.

As Nobel Laureate Daniel Kahneman put it, "For some of our most important beliefs, we have no evidence at all, except that people we love and trust hold these beliefs. Considering how little we know, the confidence we have in our beliefs is preposterous – and it is also essential."

When I consider Kahneman's use of the word preposterous, I immediately think of how some of my beliefs originate with subjective observations and half-truths. I am not implying a deliberate intent on the part of some omnipotent malevolent force to mislead me. As it turns out most of what I believe originated with those to whom I looked for love, guidance, and protection growing up and what they believed to be true and right at the time even though in some cases it was inaccurate. This confidence or blind acceptance over time becomes habitual to the point of residing in our subconscious, default mind.

Once an idea or belief takes up residency in the default mind, it burrows in so deeply into our psyche to the point of becoming a hard-wired way of thinking beyond the conscious, intentional mind's perception. It becomes nearly impossible to ferret out that belief and then change it without a deliberate and concentrated effort. In essence, it has become hidden.

Hidden In Plain Sight

Becoming conscious of the fact that you have hidden beliefs is a very important first step. Being able to consciously recognize those beliefs and reconcile their impact can prove problematic.

Once again, hidden beliefs are those ideas, values, or morals that have become second nature to you and that you accept as being true. In this regard, they are hidden in plain sight because they impact everything that you perceive, think and do but are not recognized consciously. If you have ever said to yourself; why did I do that, or why do I think the way that I do, you will understand what I mean. By identifying your hidden beliefs and their impact on your daily living, you will be answering these questions. And this is the purpose of Step #5.

When you identify your hidden beliefs, understand their impact, and challenge their continuing validity, you will then be in the position through the introduction of new mind habits, to start establishing a collaborative and productive alignment between your default mind and your intentional mind. As a result, you will be empowered with greater insight and therefore, better able to position yourself and others to succeed.

Signs of Trouble

So, how do you identify your hidden beliefs? Where is the first place you look?

A good starting point is noting your reactions in various situations.

Let's revisit my reaction when I was stuck behind a slow-moving vehicle while trying to get on the highway.

As mentioned, my reaction was one of annoyance and frustration. But, what if instead of annoyance and frustration, I became enraged and aggressive? What if I rode the bumper of the car in front of me, and repeatedly honked my horn? Then, finally gaining access to the highway, I gave the driver of the car that held me up a rude gesture and pulled away cursing at a dangerously high-speed? Would this have been an acceptable and proportional response?

If a thousand other people experienced the same thing, how would most of them react? I am sure that while some may have felt a certain degree of frustration, generally speaking, a response to the magnitude above would be considered over-the-top – and rightfully so.

Why am I sharing this alternative scenario with you?

Because a reaction that is so intense is a sure indication

that beneath the surface, and for whatever reason, what I am experiencing goes against a strong, hidden belief. Such a response is the first and usually, the most reliable indication that somehow a hidden belief that I hold near and dear has been threatened. After all, you do not get so deeply emotional for something that is not important to you. It is at this point; you must take a step back and using the signs below recognize that a hidden belief is at the heart of your thinking and subsequent response.

For greater clarity, here are the signs that a hidden belief is at work behind your reaction to a person, place, or event:

- Disproportionate reaction

- Strong, difficult emotions (rage, depression, anger, fear, hopelessness)

- A deep feeling of animosity or "allergy" towards something or someone

- Justification

Looking Beyond The Justification Trap

It is important to note that one of the most common ways to derail the hidden belief discovery process is the habit of justification.

Let's say, that to justify my over-reaction I conclude that my anger was warranted because the driver in front of me was making me late for an important meeting or did not appreciate the fact that I was rushing to visit a friend who had suddenly taken ill.

Justifications such as these seem both fair and reasonable, which is why they are a trap. In reality, your default mind uses justifications to explain away the immediate discomfort of losing control emotionally. The underlying cause is made obscured by such "explanations" and is therefore likely to result in a similar reaction in the same kind of situation should it arise again in the future.

To put it another way, when the default mind justifies its reaction, it is also justifying or defending itself regarding its alignment with an important underlying belief. It is protecting it while keeping the limiting belief safe, and isn't that the main purpose of the default mind; to keep its beliefs and therefore you safe?

For example, the root of my anger at the driver in front of

me might be my belief "I am only safe and worthwhile, i.e. job security, if I am always the first person arriving at the office before my peers." Or if I am late for a meeting with a client, I might think that I will lose the sale if I am not on time. There are always underlying threats of loss or failure tied to such hidden beliefs. As a result, I am "blinded" to the fact that the person in front of me is an older gentleman driving cautiously in a complex situation. Instead, I see him as an enemy that is trying to get in the way of my very survival – which is rather extreme. And what happens in extreme situations? My fight or flight mindset kicks in. Hence my over-the-top reaction.

The above example regarding a slow-moving vehicle will likely lead you to think that you would never react that way in a similar situation. While true for most, the critical point to remember is that all hidden beliefs follow a similar pattern regardless of their origins or how they are triggered in your everyday life. You must ask yourself, what hidden belief is tied to your slow-moving car?

Be warned that when you earnestly seek the underlying hidden beliefs behind your actions and reactions, you might have to acknowledge and accept that a long-held belief is either no longer valid or was never valid in the first place. Regarding the last point, a great deal of our current beliefs, which originated in early childhood are self-limiting as they are tied to over-compensating the safety need.

The reason why not only identifying but challenging entrenched beliefs is so difficult is because you are moving out of the security of a safe and known zone which is your way of thinking and how you perceive yourself and the world around you. When you challenge your beliefs, you are consciously choosing to step into the minefield of the unknown This is the way of having a new perspective that can, for many, be initially a frightening proposition filled with self-revelatory condemnation rather than freedom and peace of mind.

That said, and given what you have learned in Steps #1 through #4, you can now see that by challenging existing, and previously hidden beliefs, you will gain a new perspective that will free you.

Referring once again to my slow-moving driver, instead of looking at my being late as a negative fault on my part, I will consciously realize that arriving first at the office ahead of my peers does not necessarily correlate to job security. As a result of this revelation, how will my attitude toward the peers, work and the driver change? Am I likely to be more observant and therefore have empathy for the older gentleman recognizing the challenge he might be facing?

In this context, you now see that the unknown presents new and exciting opportunities for self-discovery and personal empowerment, i.e. greater emotional intelligence. With greater emotional intelligence comes the ability to gain social intelligence that is essential for your success in a VUCA world.

In my group sessions, we use reflective exercises to uncover our mind habits; however, if you are reading this book, you might find it useful to keep a reflective journal to review daily challenges. Consider how you reacted to the challenge. Where did that reaction come from? How did it impact your mood, actions or decisions for the rest of the day? Viewing the incident with a "clear "mind, what alternative actions might have been more productive? A journal is also a good safe place to contemplate your reactions to controversial VUCA issues in a changing business environment or overcoming misunderstandings with coworkers or clients from different social or ethnic backgrounds whose "favourite" default mindsets may or not be the same as your own.

In steps, #6 through #9, I will focus on how you can use your new-found emotional intelligence and inner-leadership to build stronger and mutually beneficial relationships with others.

STEP #6

EMPATHY THE WAY OF THE HEART

"Seek first to understand, then to be understood"
— Stephen Covey

Having empathy requires you to see both the forest and the trees. To get to the stage of seeing the forest, you must move beyond the myopic focus of your personal experiences and beliefs that like so many trees obfuscate your ability to comprehend the bigger picture. Specifically, you must have the ability to step outside of yourself and identify the perceptions, feelings, and underlying beliefs that drive others. Being able to have this social intelligence enables you to not only understand what makes someone else tick, but it also lays the important cornerstone of any great relationship.

You were the focus of the first five steps covered in this book. Such an approach is logical in that you must first get your own house in order before you have the right mindset to consider and understand others.

Enlightened and empowered by your new self-awareness in this chapter, we will now turn your focus outwards, starting with understanding what is and is not empathy.

Sympathy Is Not Empathy

It is not uncommon for people to confuse or use interchangeably the words sympathy and empathy. But there is a significant difference.

Feeling sympathy or sorry for someone is putting your experience first - you come first. Having empathy, on the other hand, which is a much deeper act, is putting yourself in someone else's shoes to experience what they are thinking and feeling. They come first.

Take the older gentleman driving the slow-moving car in front of me. I may have sympathy for him, in that I feel bad for him because he is old and is having difficulty navigating the high-speed on-ramp. Conversely, when I experience empathy, I move from a surface understanding to a relational one where I can imagine myself behind the wheel at that age and how daunting a task driving a car would be under such circumstances. Think of the differences between sympathy and empathy as expressing your feelings first versus expressing the thoughts and emotions of others feel first. With the latter, you gain a much deeper insight into what another person's situation is because you are in it. When you have empathy, you are "actually" walking a mile in the other person's shoes.

Your ability to not only understand but experience what others are feeling is representative of the attributes in the "creative" upper hemisphere of the previously referenced 360 Leadership Circle Profile™. Specifically, where your effective intentional leadership abilities in the relating dimension reside.

The challenge is that most leaders, in fact most people, operate from the lower hemisphere in the 360 Leadership Circle Profile™ in which a reactive mindset limits your ability to have real empathy for others because you are busy coming from a compulsive, self-driven standpoint.

When you live in a lower versus upper hemisphere mindset, your "own" safety or security comes first creating a divide between you and others. A sign of lower hemisphere isolation is your internal defensive monologue when listening to someone else in which you are thinking; "what am I going to say to look good or come across as smart and capable." As a result, you are unable to relate to what others are thinking and feeling and therefore, cannot establish meaningful relationships beyond cursory or periphery interactions which may risk you be seen as inauthentic.

While this disconnect may suggest self-centeredness, in reality, your inability to have empathy is the result of your actions and interactions being "driven" without challenge by the default mind.

To overcome this deeply embedded programming, you must make an intentional effort to look beyond the instinctive, self-driven response mechanism of the default mind through a deliberate collaboration with your conscious or intentional mind.

In the next section, I will demonstrate how to engage and collaborate with your intentional mind.

Empathy Is A Two-Way Street

"The more you give, the more you get." The underlying message of this old saying is true when it comes to empathy.

Let's consider the following exercise from my group sessions.

Exercise Synopsis: John arrived 30-minutes late to pick-up Mary for an important client call because on the way to work he had a flat tire. As he could not reach her with his cell to let her know that he would be running late. When he finally did arrive, Mary was furious, she was a stickler for punctuality and was nervous about this client visit. How could he calm her down enough to listen to what happened.

Here is the ensuing exchange between John and Mary;

Mary: "You are half an hour late! You knew that this was an important client visit and that I hate being late. Worst of all, you did not even call me to let me know that you had been delayed. I hate it when you don't consider others! What am I supposed to tell the client?"

John: "I'm sorry that I was late. I know how you hate being late to client meetings. It may seem to you I do not consider others, so I can understand your frustration."

Mary: "That's right; I feel very frustrated. So, what happened? Why are you so late?"

(Note: John's empathic comment puts into words Mary's thoughts and feelings of upset and frustration. Mirroring her feelings this way, helped calm her down. Her tone shifts from being adversarial to collaborative. As a result, Mary is more willing to hear his reason for being late, without perceiving it as an excuse.)

When John explains the flat tire and his failed attempts to reach her by cell phone, Mary's anger dissipated:

Mary: "Yes, I've had a lot of calls this morning. That's too bad about the tire it could happen to anyone. Sorry I got so angry. You know how I hate being late for appointments with a client."

There was a critical moment that could have led to an escalation of offense and hostility, causing both John and Mary to retreat into a default "fight or flight" mode. Do you know to which moment I am referring?

When Mary accused John of being inconsiderate of both her and their client's time John could have responded in one of the two following ways;

1. He could have responded defensively and with hostility accuse Mary of being unfair and selfish because he could not have foreseen his getting a flat tire, or

2. He could have remained silent but resentful, thereby closing off not only at that moment but perhaps for all time any open and productive dialogue with Mary.

Neither of the above two response options would have served the best interests of either. Although he had a justifiable reason for being late, John intentionally chose to be empathetic of Mary's position, acknowledging that he understood her reasons for being angry, before asking her to understand his reasons for being late. When that happened the exchange between Mary and John took a positive which prompted a similar empathetic response from Mary regarding John's situation.

It is important to first seek to understand before hoping to be understood.

To reach this point of empathetic engagement, John did two very important things.

To start, he first labelled the emotions in himself (refer to my session on self-awareness) which enabled him to identify with the emotions that Mary was experiencing (anger, frustration, and perhaps even a bit of worry of how the client would react) and silently repeat to himself "anger, anger", or "frustration, frustration."

Next, John was effective at constructing an empathic dialogue with Mary utilizing the following guiding principles:

1. His use of the "you" pronoun;

2. His willingness to discipline himself to pay close attention to the words Mary used to express her thoughts, feelings, desires, and expectations. while self-managing.

3. His ability to self-manage his own feelings and to reflect Mary's thoughts and feelings in his words.

The above skills are especially important for you as a leader, as it creates trust and facilitates either the understanding or buy-in of the other person.

Here is an exercise that can help you to practice empathy as it provides you with an opportunity to come up with an empathic comment to a friend in following scenarios.

1. "I got stuck in the traffic and was an hour late to the interview."

2. "I did not get the promotion."

3. "It was such an expensive restaurant and the food was not that great."

What is important to remember when practicing empathy is the following:

Deep Listening + Managing your own thoughts and feelings + Empathic Communication (i.e., putting into words what the other person is thinking or feeling).

The principles and exercises from this chapter will also assist you in other related scenarios, including giving feedback and conflict management. I will talk about both in the next two steps.

(The John & Mary scenario in this section was adapted from the book *The EQ Edge Emotional Intelligence and your success.* Steven J. Stein & Howard E. Book)

STEP #7

CONFLICT MANAGEMENT

"Conflict is inevitable; combat is optional."
— *Max Lucado*

The Center for Creative Leadership (CCL®) a top-ranked provider of executive education training puts Problems with Interpersonal Relationships as a primary career-staller for leaders. While conflict is inevitable, managing conflict inwardly and outwardly effectively is a crucial task of leadership. In this section we share specific tools and techniques for resolving inner & outer conflict effectively.

For those who have not arrived at the point of mastering steps 1 through 6, both the prospects of conflict and the outcomes have been under the influence of being in your fight or flight mindset. In other words, you are likely to perceive conflict in a negative light versus being an opportunity to gain new insights and understanding, leading to more meaningful relationships and outcomes.

Often those who seem to be in a state of confrontation perpetually do not have issues with others in the outside or real world. Instead, their battles originate within, being triggered by the default mind which tends to create internal dialogues and related expectations of what may happen based on past experiences that rarely has any connection to a present situation.

As I had indicated earlier in this book, in the majority of these instances what you expect in the way of how someone else will act or react does not usually align with reality. Unfortunately, and because of this internal dialogue, many negotiations and interactions in business and even in private life are hijacked by the fight or flight instinct that resides in the default mind.

Therefore, the key to effective conflict management is to incorporate what you have learned and practiced in the previous five steps (emotional intelligence) and, with greater empathy via Step #6, to gain a real and accurate insight into a situation in which there is misalignment of perceptions.

Within the above context, the first and most important step is to realize that conflict is inevitable and that when it occurs, it is not a reflection of you or the other person being disagreeable or unreasonable. Conflict at its core is a request for more information and greater understanding.

The Positive Side of Conflict

One of my earliest mentors had this to say about conflict; "if both of us always habitually agree on everything, then our relationship may be redundant."

While it may not initially be welcome or seen in a positive light, conflict is a valuable tool to hone ideas and forge a deeper and more meaningful dialogue leading to stronger relationships. The results of perceiving conflict in this way ultimately lead to greater transparency, i.e., tell me what you "really think," as well as an improvement in collaboration and corresponding outcomes. The key, however, is not only in your view or attitude regarding conflict, but the way that you engage with it – starting with the resolution of the conflict within.

Understanding the Battle Within

The roots of how you respond to conflict in the outside world may depend on how you habitually relate to yourself, either with self-critical or a self-compassionate tone. The difference between the two is that a self-critical tone operates within the framework of sympathetic system a threat system (fight/flight), while a care-giving or parasympathetic system directs the self-compassionate tone.

When you are self-critical:

- Your Inner-Critic wants to keep the self protected even if ineffective and detrimental;

- The physiological self-defence system then kicks in as follows:

    - Activates Amygdala – releases the stress hormone adrenaline and cortisol

    - Gears up for fight/flight to increase survival chance (useful before but not now)

When self-compassion moves the brain, it also wants to keep you safe but instead of threat system (sympathetic) it activates the care-giving system (parasympathetic), the following happens:

- Your brain releases oxytocin, which lowers cortisol and calms you down.

While both the self-criticism and self-compassion systems want to keep you safe, it is important to remember:

1. Sympathetic fight/flight system is effective for dealing with outer physical threats such as lions, fire. But, it is ineffective when dealing with problems such as weight gain, or dealing with a boss, husband/wife, or friend.

2. Self-compassion is useful when a threat is psychological (it has to do with the thoughts and images we think or what we say to ourselves) and not physical.

It is important to note that as the power of your awareness regarding inner conflicts increases you will begin to see the nature of the default habitual mind, i.e., its criticisms, judgments, fears, envy, etc. As a result, gaining this new awareness may turn up the heat of self-criticism and inner conflict. It is important to know this because, if you are not aware of what is happening, you may abandon or quit the entire 9-step practice. Ironically, the reason some people quit is not that the 9-steps do not work, but because the steps work rather well in revealing the nature of the default mind. Think of it in the context of opening a door and finally coming face-to-face with something you expected the least - your habitual self. For an example how to deal effectively with inner-conflict please refer back to "Disarming Your Default Mind."

Turning Conflict Inside-Outward

Once you understand and tame the conflict within yourself, you can more easily empathize with someone with whom you have a conflict. The reason is simple; we are all inherently similar in varying degrees regarding the influence of our default mind.

Understanding how your mind works and the differences regarding the self-critical versus the self-compassionate mind means that you can view their position and their way of expressing it in a truer light.

The next time you find yourself in a conflict, try engaging the other person as follows:

Acknowledge: "John or Mary, I can see right now you have strong feelings about this situation." *(Note: by acknowledging their feelings, you validate their right to have an opposing position without judging it or them.)*

Seek To Understand: "What is it that most concerns you regarding the situation, i.e., that you will miss an opportunity, or lose a client." *(Note: by wanting to sincerely understand what it is that concerns them you will move them from defending their position to explaining it – from fight and flight to parasympathetic. You also get an insight to what they value greatly.)*

Seek Confirmation: "Thank you for explaining to me why

you are concerned. Just so I am clear, this is your main concern or do you have other concerns?" *(Note: by seeking confirmation you not only ensure that you understand their issues with what is happening, but you are also serving as a sounding board for them as well. Often when you restate a concern back to someone, they see it in a new light. In some instances, they may even realize that the concerns they have are not as significant as it was when it was only part of their internal dialogue.)*

Create Commonality: Say to them, "I have felt the same way in other situations." *(Note: By telling them that you have also felt that way creates a bond through shared feelings in which your common human experience stimulates not only two-way empathy but opens the door to the productive, non-defensive dialogue which is critical in the conflict resolution process.)*

Using the above steps to deescalate a situation will create an atmosphere of understanding, leading to collaboration towards resolution versus a showdown. In the end, the one thing to remember is that when it comes to conflict management, there is no absolute right or wrong only different perspectives and ways of accomplishing a mutual objective.

STEP #8

GIVING FEEDBACK

In Step #8 we continue with application of new-found inner leadership and understanding of thoughts and emotions to build a stronger leadership through offering effective intentional feedback.

According to Ron Carucci in his Harvard Business Review post, *Giving Feedback to Someone Who Hasn't Had It in Years,* "Study after study shows that more than 69% of us try to sidestep communicating negative information, and 37% won't give critical feedback at all. As a result, many leaders remain clueless about how others experience them." My own experience has been that giving feedback can often be a daunting task for leaders. They may fear that their feedback will be hard to accept and that people will get emotional. At the same time, they may say something they might regret or lose the approval of others. In most of above cases, the reasons for difficulty in offering effective feedback rests upon the default way we regard ourselves. We don't want to give feedback, because being liked is very important to us. Our default mind has convinced us that in order to remain safe and secure we must be liked by people at any cost and refrain from "rocking the boat." In this way, people will not be disappointed in us and withdraw their love or care.

While this line of thinking may have served us as vulnerable children, it does not hold to the light of truth as a successful professional adult. Yet, the outmoded hidden beliefs that run the default ways of thinking and acting cannot see their own limitations. As a result there is the hesitation to offer constructive feedback or the tendency to offer a watered down version. These approaches can lead to conflict or ineffectiveness at work.

Common Feedback Mistakes:

The Centre for Creative Leadership lists *10 Common Mistakes when giving Feedback*. There are five that are particularly relevant to our discussion. As we said earlier the default mind's main objective is to keep us safe. When it comes to giving feedback, the default mind uses specific strategies to attain this goal.

1. It focuses on the person rather than their behavior (to make us right, superior and safe by making the other party wrong and inferior). This approach will usually backfire as it is likely to make the other party defensive and uncooperative.

2. It offers generalized feedback instead of objective specific feedback tied to specific behaviour and occasion, missing the opportunity for genuine tactful communication.

3. It looks to a third party to back up its feedback bringing others onside to support its opinion "John thinks that …" resulting in the other party feeling under attack on many sides.

4. Alternatively, it may try soften the key point of the feedback by couching it between positives in order not to lose the approval of the other party, this is not to say offering intentional positive feedback is wrong, if it is genuine and appropriate, but it is not helpful and may even sound insincere when it is done gratuitously.

5. It can easily get caught up in broad personal "you" statements and generalizations using with "never", and "always" terms. This approach is sure to trigger anger and defensiveness in the other party.

It is not hard to see why leaders find the experience of giving feedback so unappealing and full of potential pitfalls.

I am advising a simple formula of specific steps to help neutralize the default mind's habits and allow you to offer intentional and effective feedback.

A Formula for Giving Feedback (OAII)

Occasion "O": Describe the occasion where and when the observed behavior occurred. The more specific you can be about the when and where, the better.

"Yesterday at the meeting" (O)

Action: Help the individual understand the exact action you're talking about. Avoid interpretations and judgments, such as, "You weren't listening to me…" instead, simply describe the person's action:

"As I was talking you pushed your chair away from the desk and gazed out the window." (A)

Inner-experience (T/E/S): Share the inner-experience of the action on you. Inner-experience is the thought/emotion/sensation that you want to be known to the individual.

"I thought you were bored and uninterested" (T)

"I felt discouraged and lost focus" (E)

The "Inner-Experience" is an integral part of the effective feedback, this is the reason why Self-Awareness in Step 1, and Self-Management in Step 2, come first. Without practicing self-awareness we cannot articulate the inner-experience of what we think and feel.

We first need to understand and be able to manage what we feel, especially strong emotions like hurt or anger, before we can give intelligent objective feedback.

Intention. (I) Finally we ask:

"What was your intention?" (I)

By asking about their intention, it indicates we are aware that there are many perspectives and we want to understand theirs. That is why we had "Perception" module third. All these elements weave together nicely to facilitate the Feedback Formula (OAII)

The empathy step is crucial as it allows us to understand and recognize what the other person is feeling or thinking which can enrich our feedback giving further.

Positive Feedback

While critical feedback is hard for many, positive feedback or giving praise is equally difficult. It is important to keep the OAII formula in mind when giving positive feedback. Leaders often avoid giving positive feedback feeling it may lead to an appearance of favoritism or a special relationship. However positive feedback helps to reinforce actions and behaviors from others that you want to see continue. Done properly, it promotes initiative, creativity and a sense of pride in the individual's work and their sense of sharing the responsibility to the workplace success. By using the OAI formula, Occasion, Action, Inner-Experience, you must state the occasion on which their performance was commendable. "Yesterday during the quarterly review (O), you did a good job by maintain eye-contact and inviting feedback from everyone (A). It made everyone feel part of the team (I)." The closer your timing of feedback to the actual event the more effective the impact.

STEP #9

VISION

> The most pathetic person in the world is the person who has sight, but no vision.
>
> \- Helen Keller

In step #9 we further incorporate the intelligences of head and heart to create a compelling inside-out vision that enhances leadership effectiveness and business performance even more.

When you consider that Helen Keller was blind, deaf and, for many years, mute, you realize that vision is not a gift of the senses but one of the heart and mind.

In our everyday lives, we each make decisions about our business, work, career and social and intimate relationships.

Many of these decisions aren't the result of intentional planning or conscious choice. They are decisions by default made out of habit, impulse, social conditioning or inaction. These default choices are not a genuine reflection of what we are capable. They are instead the birth child of our default automatic thinking and they rarely achieve the results and outcomes we intended.

What is Vision?

> *Action without vision is passing time. Vision without action is fantasy - J. Barker*

Vision is a mental image that inspires sustained action. While fantasy uses imagination to escape from the present reality, vision engages creative imagination to purposefully shape it. What differentiates a visionary idea from an imaginative fantasy is its power to inspire purposeful action from day-to-day. I often witness this dramatic shift during coaching sessions with clients. When clients form a vision based on what is inwardly rewarding to them, their energy levels and their perception of their career path takes on a dramatic shift. Their vision empowers them! It has a heartbeat.

Why is Vision Important?

Without vision, we may gradually numb our senses, deny our passion and slowly settle into routine, accepting what is, rather than what can be. The dangers are clearly evident in the "Boiled Frog" example.

If you place a frog in a pot of boiling water, it will immediately try to scramble out. But if you place the frog in room temperature water, and don't scare it, it'll stay put. Now, if the pot sits on a heat source, and if you gradually turn up the temperature, something interesting happens. As the temperature initially rises from 70 to 80 degrees F., the frog will not notice it. In fact, it will show every sign of enjoying itself. As the temperature gradually increases, the frog will become groggier and dazed until it is unable to climb out of the pot. Even though nothing is restraining it, the frog will sit there and boil.

The fate of the boiled frog isn't so unlike that of individuals, leaders or organizations as they gradually laze into routine and abandon their vision and creative force.

Have I Become Complacent?

- If you could realize every last bit of your business or team potential, what would that look like?

- If for the moment there was nothing to stop you and you knew you could not possibly fail what would you do?

If there is a big gap between the current reality and your answer to above questions, it may be a sign of 'boiled frog' syndrome.

The key to moving from reaction and complacency to new results is by training the mind to move from a default state to a creative state.

Creating a Vision

There are ways to help you stimulate your creative power to develop a vision. Numerous prominent writers on change management and transformation have developed mind exercises that can assist you to promote your creativity and find your true passions. The following are sample exercises that I have found useful in my own learning path.

1. Choose an area you want to create an intentional vision for. Write your challenge

    "I feel empty inside. My life lacks meaning and purpose"

"I feel lonely and lack genuine intimacy in my life"

"I am unfulfilled and unhappy with my work"

2. Then frame your challenge as a question,

By framing the above challenge into a question, you engage the power of curiosity and inquiry.

The formulation of the question is as important as the solution. The depth of your inquiry and the range of answers you will find depends on how well you define the question. Half-hearted questions will generate incomplete answers. In a sense, questions contain the answers within them, as a seed contains the plant within itself.

Framing the question makes the whole difference. For example,

> "I am lonely and lacking genuine intimacy in my life" becomes "How can I cultivate meaningful relationships?"
>
> "I am tired of ongoing insufficient financial means" becomes "How can I uncover and tap into inner-abundance?"

"I am unfulfilled with my work" becomes "How can I serve?"

3. Contemplate the questions above until you are satisfied that genuine answers are emerging and put them into writing.

4. Your answer is your initial vision.

Vision-Quest

Spontaneously complete the endings to these statements to facilitate emergence of vision.

1. What I care about above all is …

2. What I would do if I knew I could not possibly fail and there was no limitation is …

3. To make my life and leadership a creative expression of what I most care about, I can start with …

4. I get in the way of my vision emerging when I …

Turning What Moves You Most Into A Vision

A vision is a mental image of a future outcome, which inspires us. You will know when a vision hits you by the energy and excitement you feel.

Questions for creating a vision:

1. Suppose you could wave a magic wand and have anything you want manifested for your personal/professional life, or your business? Write down your thoughts. What do you see as your role in ensuring these changes come to pass?

2. In your opinion, what are the most critical needs in your industry going unmet? What are the greatest sources of discontent and dysfunction in your industry, your business and your workplace?

3. What situations in your industry, business or workplace move you the most?

    Complete this sentence. "More than anything, I want to do something about…"

4. What situation in your industry, business or workplace do you complain about the most?

Complete this sentence. "Somebody really ought to do something about …"

Complete this sentence. "If I were to take more responsibility to do something about this, my first action would be …"

Visualizing Your Legacy

Imagine you are at your retirement party, your colleagues, friends and family surround you. You feel that you have fully accomplished the goals of your career. Write you farewell speech you might want to include answers to these questions.

1. What was the message of your life?

2. What was the guiding vision for your career?

3. What was your purpose in life?

4. What do you want to be remembered for?

5. What was your most important contribution? Why?

6. What were your most meaningful experiences? Why?

Vision Matters

We can all think of people whose visions have changed and are changing our world. The vision of a self-governing India, motivated the life work of Mahatma Gandhi. The vision of a true democracy for South Africa kept Nelson Mandela's spirit strong through years of imprisonment. The vision of a worldwide communications network spurred on Bill Gates, Steve Jobs and many others in the building of the internet, computers and electronics that have turned science fiction into reality.

Not all visions have to be monumental, but they do need to be life-affirming and free us from our real or imagined fetters. They should allow us to rise above the daily irritants or agonies that grind us down. Take the time to work through the exercises in this section to fully develop your vision and its potential for your work, your life and your community.

Letting Your Vision Take Flight

What will it take for you to find your vision? Will it be by your own will and planning or will the forces of change be so great that you have no choice. One of the participants in my group coaching sessions shared the story below.

> Once there was a king who received a gift of two magnificent falcons from Arabia. They were

peregrine falcons, the most beautiful birds he had ever seen. He gave the precious birds to his head falconer to be trained.

Months passed and one day the head falconer informed the king that though one of the falcons was flying majestically, soaring high in the sky, the other bird had not moved from its branch since the day it had arrived.

The king summoned healers and sorcerers from all the land to tend to the falcon, but no one could make the bird fly. He presented the task to the leaders of his court, but the next day, the king saw through the palace window that the bird had still not moved from its perch.

Having tried everything else, the king thought to himself, "May be I need someone more familiar with the countryside to understand the nature of this problem." So he cried out to his court, "Go and get a farmer, and let him try"

In the morning, the king was thrilled to see the falcon soaring high above the palace gardens. He said to his court, "Bring me the doer of this miracle."

The court quickly located the farmer, who came and stood before the king. The king asked him, "How did you make the falcon fly?"

With his head bowed, the farmer said to the king, "It was very easy, your highness. I simply cut the branch on which the bird was sitting."

Moral: *We are all made to fly* -- to realize our potential as human beings. But instead of doing that, we sit on our branches, clinging to the things that are familiar to us. The possibilities are endless, but for most of us, they remain undiscovered. We conform to the familiar, the comfortable, to the safety of mundane. So for the most part, our lives are mediocre instead of exciting, thrilling and fulfilling.

> *"where as the average individuals often have not the slightest idea of what they are, of what they want, of what their own opinions are, self-actualising individuals have superior awareness of their own impulses, desires, opinions and subjective reactions in general"* - A. Maslow

Why is your "branch" holding you back? What would inspire you to soar?

It's time to spread your wings.

BIBLIOGRAPHY OF TEXTS, PROGRAMS, VIDEOS AND RESOURCES

Abraham Maslow, Hierarchy of Needs, paper 1943, "A Theory of Human Motivation" and his subsequent book *Motivation and Personality*.

Frederic LaLoux, *Reinventing Organizations* A Teal organization is an emerging organizational paradigm that advocates a level of consciousness including all previous world views within the operations of an organization.

Daniel Goleman, psychologist and author of *Emotional Intelligence*.

Robert Keegan, *Immunity to Change* Professor in Adult Learning and Professional Development at Harvard Graduate School of Education for 40 years.

Vedanta is the most prominent of six schools of Hindu Philosophy rising from the *Upanishads* focused specifically knowledge and liberation.

Charles Swindoll, *The Great Awakening*. Evangelical pastor and educator.

Jon_Kabat Zinn, *Mindfullness Based Stress Management Workshops* Centre for Mindfulness in Medicine, Healthcare & Society, University of Massachusetts, US.

Kelly McGonigal, *The Neuroscience of Change*: A compassion-based program for personal transformation.

Claus Otto Scharmer, *Presence*, Exploring Profound Change in People, Organizations, and Society

Allan Wallace, *The Attention Revolution*

Hafiz of Persia, *"The Gift"* Poems of Hafiz, Sufi poet and theosopher.

Eric Butterworth, "The Law of Visualization", *Spiritual Economics*

Choiceless Awareness, J.Krishnamurti in the video series : *J. Krishnamurti, David Bohm, The Future of Humanity*.

Mokokoma Mokhonoana, *Divided and Conquered*, South African philosopher and social critic.

The 360 Leadership Circle Profile is an assessment tool that measures the creative competencies and the reactive tendencies of leaders. http://leadershipcircle.com

Anurag Shourie, Author of *Half a Shadow*. Executive Search Consultant at Leaders International.

Daniel Kahneman, *Thinking, Fast and Slow,* 2002 Nobel Laureate in Economic Sciences

Stephen Covey, *7 Habits of Highly Effective People,* businessman and speaker.

Steven J. Stein & Howard E. Book, *The EQ Edge, Emotional Intelligence and Your Success.*

Max Lucado, author of *Anxious for Nothing.*

Ron Carucci, web post *Giving Feedback to Someone Who Hasn't had it in Years* in the Harvard Business Review

https://hbr.org/2020/01/giving-feedback-to-someone-who-hasnt-had-it-in-years

The Centre for Creative Leadership *10 Common Mistakes in Giving Feedback*

https://www.ccl.org/multimedia/video/10-common-mistakes-in-giving-feedback/

Joel Barker, *Discovering the Future: The Business of Paradigms*

Ravi Gupta, *MBA, Through Stories: The Art of Effective Management Through 44 Enriching Tales.*

ABOUT THE AUTHOR

Kamran Tork is an experienced Executive Coach, with over 20 years of international work experience in diverse functions including operations, consulting and coaching in Canada, Malaysia and UAE. His core expertise lies in the development of human engagement to enhance organizational performance. He has a deep interest in the areas of executive career coaching, emotional intelligence and mindfulness practices for leadership and professionals.

Kamran Tork received his degree in Economics from the University of Toronto, Canada. He has been certified in a number of leadership development assessment tools. He is a Professional Certified Coach PCC from the International Coach Federation ICF.

He moved to Dubai in 2008 where he pioneered the

introduction of Mindfulness/Self-Reflective Practices to leadership development programs. Over the years since, Kamran Tork has been working on number of leadership development initiatives with renowned business schools and large international organizations providing executive coaching support to mid-senior level clients.

From his base in Dubai, Kamran Tork has coached and supported clients globally including Insead Business School, Roche, Merck Serono, Weatherford, Nokia, LinkedIn, London Business School, HSBC, Nissan, Richemont, Lee Hecht Harrison, Votorantim Cimentos, J&J, Pepsi, Microsoft, Nestle, ADIA, Serco, Center for Creative Leadership, MBRPLD, and Ashridge Business School to name a few.

www.ingramcontent.com/pod-product-compliance
Lightning Source LLC
Chambersburg PA
CBHW031920240526
45464CB00021B/616